HOW TO WRITE YOUR OWN LIVING WILL

HOW TO WRITE YOUR OWN LIVING WILL

with forms

———

Edward A. Haman
Attorney at Law

Sourcebooks
Inc.

Naperville, IL • Clearwater, FL

Published by: **Sourcebooks, Inc.**

Naperville Office
P.O. Box 372
Naperville, Illinois 60566
(630) 961-3900
FAX: 630-961-2168

Clearwater Office
P.O. Box 25
Clearwater, Florida 33757
(813) 587-0999
FAX: 813-586-5088

Cover Design: Andrew Sardina/Dominique Raccah
Interior Design and Production: Andrew Sardina, Sourcebooks, Inc.

This publication is designed to provide accurate and authoritative information in regard to the subject matter covered. It is sold with the understanding that the publisher is not engaged in rendering legal, accounting, or other professional service. If legal advice or other expert assistance is required, the services of a competent professional person should be sought.

From a Declaration of Principles Jointly Adopted by a Committee of the
American Bar Association and a Committee of Publishers and Associations

Library of Congress Cataloging-in-Publication Data

Haman, Edward A.
    How to write your own living will : with forms / Edward A. Haman.
        p. cm.
    Includes index.
    ISBN 1-57071-167-4 (pbk.)
    1. Right to die--Law and legislation--United States--States--Popular works. I. Title.
KF3827.E87H356   1997
344.73'04197--dc21

97-22847
CIP

Printed and bound in the United States of America.

Paperback — 10 9 8 7 6 5 4 3 2 1

CONTENTS

Using Self-Help Law Books

Whenever you shop for a product or service, you are faced with various levels of quality and price. In deciding what product or service to buy, you make a cost/value analysis. You weigh your willingness to pay against the quality you desire.

When buying a car, you decide whether you want transportation, comfort, status, or sex appeal. Accordingly, you decide among such choices as a Neon, a Lincoln, a Rolls Royce, or a Porsche. Before making a decision, you usually weigh the merits of each option against the cost.

When you get a headache, you can take a pain reliever (such as aspirin) or see a medical specialist for a neurological examination. Given this choice, most people take a pain reliever, since it costs only pennies, whereas a medical examination costs hundreds of dollars and takes a lot of time. This is usually a logical choice because rarely is anything more than a pain reliever needed for a headache. But in some cases, a headache may indicate a brain tumor, and failing to see a specialist right away can result in complications. Should everyone with a headache go to a specialist? Of course not. But people treating their own illness must realize they are betting, based on their analysis of the situation, that they are taking the most logical option.

The same cost/value analysis must be made in deciding to do one's own legal work. Many legal situations are very straightforward, requiring a simple form and no complicated analysis. Anyone with a little intelligence and a book of instructions can handle the matter without outside help.

But there is always the chance that complications are involved that only an attorney would notice. To simplify the law into a book like this, several legal cases often must be condensed into a single sentence or paragraph. Otherwise, the book would be several hundred pages long and too complicated for most people. However, this simplification necessarily leaves out many details and nuances that would apply to special or unusual situations. Also, there are many ways to interpret most legal questions. Your case may come before a judge who disagrees with this analysis.

Therefore, in deciding to use a self-help law book and to do your own legal work, you must realize that you are deciding that the chance your case will not turn out to your satisfaction is outweighed by the money you will save in doing it yourself. Most people handling their own simple legal matters never have a problem, but occasionally people find that it ended up costing them more to have an attorney straighten out the situation than it would have if they had hired an attorney in the beginning. Keep this in mind while handling your case, and be sure to consult an attorney if you feel you might need further guidance.

INTRODUCTION

This book is designed to enable you to prepare your own living will without hiring a lawyer. It will explain the law regarding living wills, guide you in deciding which form you need, and show you how to prepare it. Be sure to read the previous section on "Using Self-Help Law Books."

The difficulty in covering any area of law on a national scale is that the law is different in each state. However, the general type of information found in most living wills is very similar in each state. Appendix A of this book will give you some information about your state's specific laws. Many states have officially approved forms. These forms are found in Appendix B, along with general forms for use in any state that does not have its own form.

The old saying that "knowledge is power" is especially true in the law. Lawyers have worked hard for many years to make the law complicated, so that only they have the knowledge and the power. This book will give you a fair amount of knowledge so that you can take back some of the power. By reading this book, you will know as much about living wills as most recent law school graduates, and will probably know more than many.

Read this entire book (including the listing for your state in Appendix A) before you prepare any papers. This will give you the information you need to decide what form to use and how to fill it out. You may also want to visit your local law library to get more information. The section on "Legal Research" in Chapter 3 will help you.

To complete the necessary form, you will need to use the general information in the main part of this book, consult the listing for your state in Appendix A, read any instructions on the form itself, and use the information from any additional reading and research. If you need to refer back to this book for answers to specific questions, use the Table of Contents and the Index to help locate the answers you need.

Living Wills and Related Documents

1

The subject of living wills is not pleasant, but it cannot be avoided if one is to face the realities of life. With the advances in medical science, it is often possible to keep someone technically alive indefinitely. Instead of allowing terminally ill patients to die a natural death, many are kept "alive" by the use of drugs and machines. A situation can also arise where a person becomes permanently unconscious, but is not going to die as long as food and water are provided. Either condition can place a burden, both emotionally and financially, upon the person's loved ones. Many people would prefer to be allowed to die, rather than exist in such a state. A lot of us feel that such an existence would be pointless, and lacking of any quality of life.

Many other people believe that all human life is sacred, and that life should be preserved at all cost. Still others believe that certain steps should be taken to preserve life, but other steps should not be taken. An individual's views on this subject are often deeply tied to the person's moral and religious beliefs. Regardless of the view you take, it may one day be important that your family members and doctors know how you feel. You can make your beliefs known through a living will.

A living will is simply a paper in which you explain your desires in the event certain medical conditions arise and you are not able to express your wishes at that time. A living will is usually limited to the refusal of, or desire for, certain medical treatment in the event of a terminal illness or injury (and possibly in the event of becoming permanently unconscious). In the event you are unable to communicate your desires in such situations, and don't have a living will, doctors or hospitals may decide they are legally obligated to perform certain procedures which you may not desire. If your spouse or adult child is called upon to make a decision about your care, he or she may find it helpful if you have expressed your wishes in a living will. A living will tells others what you want to happen in certain circumstances. You may see a "living will" called by other names, such as a "declaration regarding life-prolonging procedures," an "advance directive," or simply a "declaration."

DEFINITIONS   It is helpful to know some commonly used terms in order to understand living wills. The definitions below are not technical legal definitions, since they may be defined differently in various states or not defined at all. Nor are they technical medical definitions. Rather, they are general definitions to help you understand the ideas they express, regardless of how they may be specifically defined legally or medically.

☛ "Agent." A person given authority by a power of attorney.

☛ "Artificial nutrition and hydration." The use of "feeding tubes" (either through the mouth, nose, or intravenously) to provide food and water to a person unable to eat and drink normally.

☛ "Attorney-at-law." A person licensed to practice law before state or federal courts. The term has no relationship to a power of attorney or an attorney-in-fact.

☛ "Attorney-in-fact." The person given authority by a power of attorney. This is another term for "agent," and is used in many statutes. An attorney-in-fact does not have the power to represent anyone in court or to give legal advice.

☛ "Durable Power of Attorney." This is simply a power of attorney which continues after the principal becomes incapacitated.

- ☞ "Execute." To sign a legal document in the legally required manner, thereby making it valid and effective.

- ☞ "Life-prolonging procedures." Medical procedures applied to a person with a terminal illness or injury in order to delay death. Examples are machines used to maintain respiration and blood circulation. May also be called "life sustaining procedures."

- ☞ "Persistent vegetative state." This is the term frequently used to describe the situation where a person is unconscious, or in a coma, and has virtually no hope of regaining consciousness. It may also be referred to by other terms, such as "permanently unconscious" or "permanently comatose."

- ☞ "Power of Attorney." A document which gives one person (the "agent" or "attorney-in-fact") authority to act on behalf of another person (the "principal"). Traditionally, a power of attorney relates to financial matters, but now there are also health care powers of attorney (these will be discussed more below).

- ☞ "Principal." This is the person who signs (executes) a living will or power of attorney.

- ☞ "Proxy." Another term for "agent."

- ☞ "Terminal illness or injury." An illness or injury that is extremely likely to result in death.

DIFFERENCE FROM A TRADITIONAL WILL

A traditional will expresses what you want to happen to your property (and any minor children) if you die. A ***living*** will expresses what you want to happen to you (in the way of medical treatment) while you are still alive.

DIFFERENCE FROM A HEALTH CARE POWER OF ATTORNEY

In addition to a living will, you should also be aware of another type of document that can be of help in these difficult situations. That document is a "health care power of attorney." A health care power of attorney gives someone you trust (usually a family member or close friend) the authority to make decisions about your medical treatment. You may also see this referred to as a "durable power of attorney for health care," "health care proxy," "designation of health care surrogate," "advance health care directive," or some similar name.

Just as several states have created official living will forms, several have also created official health care power of attorney forms. Some of these health care power of attorney forms also include living will provisions. (Health care powers of attorney are covered in detail in the *The Power of Attorney Handbook*, by Edward A. Haman. If you live in New York, see *New York Power of Attorney Handbook*, by William P. Coyle and Edward A. Haman. If you live in Florida, see *Florida Power of Attorney Handbook*, by Edward A. Haman. These books are also published by Sourcebooks, Inc./Sphinx.)

A health care power of attorney goes farther than a living will. A living will simply says: "If I am terminally ill (or permanently unconscious) and can't tell my doctors what I want, then this is what I want done." The big restriction with a living will is that it only applies if you are terminally ill (or permanently unconscious). If you are only temporarily unconscious or otherwise unable to communicate, but are ***not*** terminally ill, a living will is of no use. You would need a health care power of attorney to cover such a situation.

With a health care power of attorney, you give another person the power to make decisions about your medical treatment if you are unable to communicate, even if you are ***not*** terminally ill or permanently unconscious. This would include approving and giving consent to surgery or other treatment.

Of course a living will may be used along with a health care power of attorney, and may even be included in the power of attorney, as a guide for the person making decisions on your behalf.

One reason some people prefer a living will to a health care power of attorney is that there may not be anyone they want to give the type of authority granted by a power of attorney.

DOCUMENTS
FOR THE BEST
PROTECTION

To be completely covered, you would be well-advised to have all of the following documents:

1. Living Will—to tell your doctors and other health care providers (and your health care agent if you also have a health care power of attorney) what your wishes are if you become terminally ill or permanently unconscious.

2. Health Care Power of Attorney—to give a trusted close relative or friend the power to make all types of health care decisions if you are unable to do so.

3. Durable Power of Attorney—to give a trusted close relative or friend the ability to handle your financial matters if you become incapacitated. Great caution must be used here, because the person you name as your agent could take your money and other property if he or she is dishonest.

4. Will—to be sure your property goes to whom you wish to have it, and to provide for the care and custody of any minor children.

LIVING WILL
CHOICES

In its most basic form, a living will merely says "If I become terminally ill or injured, I do not want any artificial means used that will only delay my death." This is still the basic form in many states that have created living will forms. Over the years, more issues have arisen, resulting in slightly more complex forms. These issues include conditions of permanent unconsciousness (where death is not imminent), distinctions between various types of medical procedures, providing food and water through feeding tubes or intravenously, alternate provisions or exceptions if the person is pregnant, and where the person ***does*** want all possible measures taken to preserve life. Such provisions have been included in the forms approved by some states. These choices will be discussed more in later chapters.

LAWYERS 2

DO YOU NEED A LAWYER?

The answer to this question will depend upon whom you ask. If you ask a lawyer, he or she may say that you definitely need one. However, the law regarding living wills is fairly simple, and by the time you are finished reading this book you will know as much as many lawyers about how to prepare a living will.

The purpose of a living will is simply to express your desires. A living will needs to accurately reflect your wishes, and meet the legal requirements for it to be honored by health care providers. Living will forms are often available from various senior citizen and other activist groups, however, these may not follow the form approved by the legislature of your state. The way most lawyers would approach this is to first consult your state laws to see if there is an approved form. If not, he or she would possibly consult a book such as this one, look at examples of other living wills (that either he or other lawyers have prepared), and prepare a document to fit your situation. That is exactly what this book will enable you to do for yourself. Actually, there are very few variables to living will forms.

One of the first questions you may have about a lawyer, and most likely the reason you are reading this book, is: How much will an attorney cost? Attorneys come in all ages, shapes, sizes, sexes, racial and ethnic groups—and price ranges. For a very rough estimate, you can probably expect an attorney to charge anywhere from $75 to $300 per hour. Most will prepare a living will for a flat fee; probably between $20 and $75. If you and your spouse each want a living will, the cost will double. Of course, a lawyer may then also suggest that you have a health care power of attorney and update your will, which could involve considerably higher costs. There are also books available to show you how to prepare these documents yourself.

If you decide to hire a lawyer, the remainder of this chapter will help you to select and work with him or her more effectively. (As the preparation of a living will is fairly simple, some of the following information is only applicable to more complicated legal matters. This information is provided in the hope it may help you in the event you ever need a lawyer for a more complex situation.)

SELECTING A LAWYER

Selecting a lawyer is a two-step process. First you need to decide which attorney to make an appointment with, then you need to decide if you want to hire that attorney.

FINDING
POSSIBLE
LAWYERS

☛ Ask a friend to recommend a lawyer he or she has hired and was happy with.

☛ Lawyer Referral Service. You can find a lawyer by looking in the Yellow Pages phone directory under "Attorney Referral Services" or "Attorneys." This is a service, usually operated by a bar association, that is designed to match a client with an attorney handling cases in the area of law the client needs. The referral service does not guarantee the quality of work, the level of experience, or the ability of the attorney.

☛ Yellow Pages. Check under the heading for "Attorneys" in the Yellow Pages phone directory. You may also find display ads indicating attorneys' areas of practice.

☛ Ask another lawyer you know, or have used in the past for some other matter, if he or she handles living wills, or could refer you to an attorney who does.

EVALUATING A LAWYER

You should select three to five lawyers from your search worthy of further consideration. Your first step will be to call each attorney's office, explain that you are interested in having a living will prepared, and ask the following questions:

☛ Does the attorney (or firm) handle preparation of a living will?

☛ How much can you expect it to cost?

☛ How soon can you get an appointment?

If you like the answers you get, ask if you can speak to the attorney. Some offices will permit this, but others will require you to make an appointment. Make the appointment if that is required. Once you get in contact with the attorney (either on the phone or at the appointment), ask the following questions:

☛ How much will it cost, and how will the fee be paid?

☛ How long has the attorney been in practice?

☛ Has the attorney handled this type of matter before?

☛ How long will it take to get a document prepared?

If you get acceptable answers to these questions, it's time to ask yourself the following questions about the lawyer:

☛ Do you feel comfortable talking to the lawyer?

☛ Is the lawyer friendly toward you?

☛ Does the lawyer seem confident in himself or herself?

☞ Does the lawyer seem to be straightforward with you, and able to explain things so you understand?

You probably have a lawyer you'll be able to work with if you get satisfactory answers to all of these questions. Most clients are happiest using an attorney with whom they feel comfortable.

WORKING WITH A LAWYER

In general, you will work best with your attorney if you keep an open, honest, and friendly attitude. You should also consider the following suggestions (these are applicable, to at least some extent, regardless of the type of legal question involved).

ASK QUESTIONS   If you want to know something or if you don't understand something, ask your attorney. If you don't understand the answer, tell your attorney and ask him or her to explain it again. There are points of law that even many lawyers don't fully understand, so you shouldn't be embarrassed to ask questions. Many people who say they had a bad experience with a lawyer either didn't ask enough questions, or had a lawyer who wouldn't take the time to explain things to them. If your lawyer isn't taking the time to explain what he or she is doing, it may be time to look for a new lawyer.

GIVE COMPLETE INFORMATION   Anything you tell your attorney is confidential. An attorney can lose his or her license to practice for revealing information without your permission. So don't hold back information.

ACCEPT REALITY   Listen to what your lawyer tells you about the law and the legal system, and accept it. It will do you no good to argue because the law or the system doesn't work the way you think it should. And remember: It's not your attorney's fault that the system isn't perfect, or that the law doesn't say what you'd like it to say.

BE PATIENT   Don't expect your lawyer to return your phone call within an hour. He or she may not be able to return it the same day either. Most lawyers are very busy, and overworked. It is rare that an attorney can maintain a full caseload and still make each client feel as if he is the only client.

TALK TO THE SECRETARY

Your lawyer's secretary can be a valuable source of information, so be friendly and get to know him or her. Often he or she will be able to answer your questions and you won't get a bill for the time.

KEEPING YOUR CASE MOVING

Many lawyers operate on the old principle of "The squeaking wheel gets the oil." Work on a case tends to get put off until a deadline is near, an emergency develops, or the client calls. There is a very good reason for this. After many years of education (and the expense of that education), lawyers hope to earn the income due a professional. This is difficult with a great many attorneys competing for clients and the high cost of office overhead. Many lawyers find it necessary to take more cases than can be effectively handled in order to make an acceptable living. That is why many attorneys work 65 hours a week or more. Your task is to become a squeaking wheel that doesn't squeak so much that the lawyer wants to avoid you. Whenever you talk to your lawyer ask the following questions:

- ☞ What is the next step?

- ☞ When do you expect it to be done?

- ☞ When should I talk to you next?

If you don't hear from the lawyer when you expect, call him or her the following day. Don't remind him or her that your call wasn't returned; just ask how things are going.

HOW TO SAVE MONEY

Of course you don't want to spend unnecessary money for an attorney. Here are a few things you can do to avoid excess legal fees:

- ☞ Don't make unnecessary phone calls to your lawyer.

- ☞ Give information to the secretary whenever possible.

- ☞ Direct your question to the secretary first. He or she will refer it to the attorney if he or she can't answer it.

☛ Plan your phone calls so you can get to the point, and take less of your attorney's time. Write down an outline if necessary.

☛ Do some of the "leg work" yourself. Pick up and deliver papers yourself, for example. Ask your attorney what you can do to assist him or her.

☛ Be prepared for appointments. Have all related papers with you, plan your visit to get to the point, and make an outline of what you want to discuss and what questions you want to ask.

PAY YOUR ATTORNEY BILL WHEN IT'S DUE

No client gets prompt attention like a client who pays his or her lawyer on time. However, you are entitled to an itemized bill, showing what the attorney did and how much time it took. If your attorney asks for money in advance, you should be sure that you and the lawyer agree on what is to be done for this fee.

FIRING YOUR LAWYER

If you find that you can no longer work with your lawyer, or don't trust your lawyer, it is time to either go it alone or get a new attorney. You will need to send your lawyer a letter stating that you no longer desire his or her services, and are discharging him or her from your case. Also state that you will be coming by his or her office the following day to pick up your file. The attorney does not have to give you his or her own notes or other work he or she has in progress, but he or she must give you the essential contents of your file (such as copies of papers already prepared and billed for, and any documents you provided). If he or she refuses to give your file to you, for any reason, contact your state's bar association about filing a complaint or "grievance" against the lawyer. Of course, you will need to settle any remaining fees owed.

THE LAW CONCERNING LIVING WILLS 3

IN GENERAL

The basics of the law concerning living wills is fairly simple. By signing a living will you are telling your family, doctors, hospital, and other health care providers what type of health care you want (or don't want) in certain situations.

The law provides that other people may rely on your wishes as expressed in your living will, and will not be legally responsible for honoring those wishes. For example, suppose you state in your living will that you do not want artificial life support procedures used if your condition is terminal. Your doctor will not be subject to a lawsuit by your estate or family for discontinuing life support procedures. Without a living will, the doctor or hospital may be reluctant to discontinue such artificial life support procedures.

The basic reason for having a living will is to get some third party (usually a doctor or hospital) to do, or not do, certain things if you become terminally ill or injured, or become permanently unconscious. The concern of the doctor is that he or she may be held liable, either civilly or criminally, for not performing a medical procedure that some could argue would have allowed you to live longer. Many states have passed laws that allow a doctor to honor a living will without being subject to any liability.

In states that do not have such a law, it may be more difficult to get a doctor to follow your living will instructions. In such cases it is important that you discuss your wishes with your spouse, family members, or friends, so that someone is fully aware of how you feel. They may then be willing to seek a court order to end artificial life support procedures, and the living will can be used to convince the judge of your wishes.

Some states have laws that authorize certain family members to make these life and death health care decisions even without a living will. However, it would probably be easier for your family members to make such decisions if they were certain how you feel about the subject. A living will can clearly express your desires.

THE LAW IN YOUR STATE

Many states have established approved forms for living wills (and health care powers of attorney). Some are separate living will forms, and others are living will provisions within a health care power of attorney form. First, refer to the listing for your state in Appendix A of this book, which will tell you about the living will laws in your state, which form to use from Appendix B, and where to locate your state's laws if you wish to do further reading. You will then locate the proper form in Appendix B and complete it.

State forms can vary in a few areas. These variations are discussed below.

TYPE OF
CONDITIONS

There are several types of situations that may be covered in a living will. Some state forms refer to only one situation, while others include two of more. The following is a brief explanation of these situations, including where problems occur in the language of some state forms (where necessary, these matters will be discussed in more detail in each state's listing in Appendix A):

1. Terminal conditions. In some states, this may be called "terminal illness" or "terminal injury," and may also be accompanied

by further language in an attempt to clearly describe the situation. In many state forms you will find language to the effect that the condition must be "incurable or irreversible," or that death must be likely to occur "within a relatively short period of time." In most cases, there is no definition of what constitutes "a relatively short period of time." In practice, this is left to the doctors to determine.

In a few states, the language of the form requires that it must be determined that the person will die "***whether or not*** life-sustaining procedures are utilized." One of the central purposes of a living will is to allow the person to die where life-sustaining procedures could keep him or her alive indefinitely. To require death to be imminent even if life-sustaining procedures are used defeats the whole purpose of the living will. This is probably just a case of poor drafting of the form. The intent of the legislature was probably to say, as the Texas form provides, that "death is imminent or will result within a relatively short time ***without*** the application of life-sustaining procedures." In practice, the poor drafting of these forms will probably be overlooked, and the obvious intent will be recognized. However, if a doctor with a lawyer's mind, or an attorney for a hospital of the doctor, ever reads the state form carefully, problems may arise in getting your living will enforced. It is still advisable to use the official form for your state, as it will probably be quickly recognized and followed by doctors and hospitals. To provide clarification of these poorly drafted forms, you may wish to use Form 46 along with the official form for your state. Form 46 gives you options to select that may better explain your desires. Form 46 also states that it is for the purpose of clarifying and detailing your desires; and provides that if it, or any part of it, is determined to be legally invalid, the remainder of the living will remains in effect.

2. Permanent unconsciousness. This is generally where the person is in a coma and not likely to recover. This may also be called a "persistent vegetative state," being "permanently comatose," having "permanent loss of the ability to communicate concerning medical treatment decisions," or similar language. In several state forms the language appears to also require the person's condition to be terminal, while in other states this is a sufficient basis on which to invoke the living will even if the person's condition is ***not*** terminal.

3. Where the burdens of treatment outweigh the benefits. This basis for invoking a living will is only available in a few states. It does not require a terminal condition.

4. Two other bases for invoking a living will are available in Oregon. These are where the person has an "advanced progressive illness" (this is defined in the official state form), and where the use of life support would cause "permanent and severe pain" and would not help the person's condition.

As a practical matter, the factors listed in 3 and 4 above will usually be connected with a very serious condition that will be either terminal or permanent unconsciousness.

FOOD AND
WATER

Some state forms have provisions relating to artificially provided food and water, also referred to as "nutrition and hydration." Some forms are silent on this subject, some require it to be provided, others include it as part of the life-sustaining procedures that will be withheld or withdrawn, and others give various types of options to select. If your state's form does not include a provision about food and water, or you do not like the choices available in your state's form, you may want to complete Form 46 and attach it to your state's form.

DOCTOR
CERTIFICATION

A question may arise as to when a person meets the qualifications to invoke his or her living will. For example, if a person must be either in a terminal condition or permanently unconscious, how is it determined whether he or she is in a terminal condition or permanently unconscious?

Some states are silent on this subject, and others require one or more doctors to certify that the circumstances exist. See your state's listing in Appendix A for the certification requirements of your state.

WITNESSES AND NOTARIES

States differ as to their requirements for how the living will must be signed. All require the person making the living will to sign it. What differs is who must witness the person sign. Depending upon the state, the required witnesses may be: 1) two or more witnesses, 2) two witnesses and a notary public, 3) either two witnesses or a notary public. Where both witnesses and a notary are required, some states only require the maker's signature to be notarized, while others require notarization of the signatures of the maker and both witnesses. Regardless of what may be required in your state, it is strongly suggested that you have two witnesses, and that your signature and your witnesses' signatures all be notarized. This may be an extra precaution if it is not legally required in your state, but it may make doctors and hospitals more likely to honor your living will without question. See your state's listing in Appendix A for the requirements of your particular state.

PREGNANCY

Another issue may arise where a person whose medical condition would call for the implementation of their living will is pregnant. Many state forms do not address this situation. Most states that do address this situation provide that the living will is temporarily invalid, or suspended, during the duration of the pregnancy. In such states, all efforts are made to keep the person alive until the child can be born, regardless of the wishes of the person. The forms for Arizona and Maryland have optional provisions to cover pregnancy.

OTHER VARIATIONS

There are various other matters that may be covered in living will forms. These include designating a person to see that your living will is honored; authorizing organ donation; expressing wishes regarding an autopsy; requesting that all efforts be made to preserve life; designating which procedures are, or are not, desired; specific revocation provisions; and designating a primary physician. Such matters will be mentioned in the listing for your state in Appendix A.

Generally you should not need to go beyond the information in this book, however, if you wish to study your state's law on living wills or health care powers of attorney, the next section of this chapter will give you more information about using the law library.

LEGAL RESEARCH

After reading this book, you may want to visit your local law library. One can usually be found at your county courthouse, or at a law school. Don't hesitate to ask the law librarian to help you find what you need. The librarian cannot give you legal advice, but can show you where to find your state's laws and other books on living wills. Some typical sources are discussed below.

STATUTES OR CODE   The main source of information is the set of books containing your state's laws. These are the "statutes," or "code," of your state ("Florida Statutes," "Mississippi Code," etc.). The title of the books may also include words such as "Revised," or "Annotated." ("Annotated California Code," "Kentucky Revised Statutes," etc.). "Revised" means updated, and "annotated" means the books contain information which explains and interprets the laws. Titles may also include the publisher's name, such as "*Purdon's* Pennsylvania Consolidated Statutes Annotated." The listing in Appendix A gives the title of the set of laws for your state. A few states have more than one set of laws, by various publishers (such as "Michigan Statutes Annotated" and "Michigan Compiled Laws Annotated").

Each year the legislature meets and changes the law, therefore, it is important to be sure you have the most current version. The most common way to update laws is with a soft-cover supplement, found in the back of each volume. There will be a date on the cover to tell you when it was published (such as "1998 Cumulative Supplement"). Other ways laws are updated is with a supplement volume, which will be found at the end of the regular set of volumes; or a looseleaf binding, in which pages are removed and replaced, or a supplement section added, as the law changes. Checking the most current law is probably all you will need. The following sources may be helpful if you want to go further:

PRACTICE MANUALS

A practice manual is a book or set of books containing detailed information about various areas of the law. They usually include forms for all different situations.

DIGESTS

A digest is a set of books giving summaries of appeals court cases. A digest for your state is best (such as "Florida Digest" or "Texas Digest"), as the national digest is difficult to use. Look in the index for the subject, such as "Living Wills," "Advance Directives," "Life-prolonging procedures," "Health Care Power of Attorney," etc.

REPORTERS

Reporters contain the full written opinions of the appeals court cases. The cases in the reporters are arranged according to dates they were decided, not according to subject matter. Therefore, you will need to use another source, such as a digest or a legal encyclopedia, to find relevant cases in the reporters.

LEGAL ENCYCLOPEDIA

A legal encyclopedia is used just like a regular encyclopedia: look up the subject you want (such as "Living Wills," or "Health Care Power of Attorney"), in alphabetical order. *American Jurisprudence* and *Corpus Juris Secundum* are the major sets, and some states have their own, such as *Florida Jurisprudence*.

WRITING YOUR LIVING WILL 4

A living will is simply a written statement that expresses your wishes to others regarding the use of specifically defined "life-prolonging procedures" in the event you become terminally ill or injured, or permanently unconscious.

LIVING WILL CHOICES

Living wills only relate to certain situations, usually where a person has an injury or illness that is fairly certain to result in death, or where the person is in a persistent vegetative state. They typically provide that a doctor must determine that death is fairly certain, or that the person is in a persistent vegetative state with no hope of recovery. Once this occurs, the living will tells your doctor, hospital, and other health care providers (and your health care agent, if you have one) what types of medical procedures you do, or do not, want.

Originally, living will forms were merely statements that a person did not want life-prolonging procedures if he or she became terminally ill or injured. All that was needed was for the person to fill in his or her name, and sign and date the form. Sometimes they were also signed by witnesses, and sometimes they were notarized. Some of the forms approved by state legislatures are still of this simple nature.

Over the years it became apparent that this was a somewhat more complicated situation, and forms were developed to cover a wider range of possibilities. Many forms now allow you to make choices on matters such as:

- ☞ Including coverage for a persistent vegetative state, even if the person's condition is not terminal.

- ☞ Being able to specify which medical procedures you do, or do not, want.

- ☞ Determining the use of artificial nutrition and hydration (i.e., the use of gastric tubes and intravenous feeding).

- ☞ Being able to state that you *do* want life-prolonging procedures.

- ☞ Having spaces for you to write in any other specific instructions or wishes regarding your medical treatment.

Some of the forms approved by state legislatures have one or more of these features. If your state's form does not include a provision you would like, you can either write it in on the state form, attach a sheet of paper with the additional provision, use Form 46 in the Appendix, or use the various forms in this book as guides for preparing your own custom form. Just be sure to use the signature, witness, and notary formats found on the form for your state (or use Form 45).

ARTIFICIAL NUTRITION AND HYDRATION

The most common question is whether to provide the person with food and water. If the person will quickly die without artificial means to maintain heart or lung function, then providing food and water will not be an issue. However, this may become important if the person is not likely to die, or not likely to die soon. Most people want to be as comfortable as possible, even if they want to be allowed to die. Withholding food or water can cause additional pain. Some people are willing to accept this pain in order to hasten death (and overall relief), whereas others would rather live a little longer if it means avoiding pain. You will find this option in many of the forms in the appendix. To decide which option is for you, it would be a good idea to discuss the matter with your doctor, a nurse, or other health care professional.

STATE FORMS   Many states have adopted specific living will forms, which are usually very similar. The following states have such statutory forms:

- Alabama
- Alaska
- Arizona
- Arkansas
- Colorado
- Connecticut
- Delaware
- Florida
- Hawaii
- Idaho
- Illinois
- Indiana
- Iowa

- Kentucky
- Louisiana
- Maine
- Maryland
- Mississippi
- Missouri
- Montana
- Nebraska
- Nevada
- New Hampshire
- New Mexico
- North Carolina
- North Dakota

- Oklahoma
- Oregon
- Rhode Island
- South Carolina
- South Dakota
- Tennessee
- Texas
- Utah
- Vermont
- Washington
- West Virginia
- Wyoming

Forms specific for these states are found in Appendix B. Many of these forms have instructions right on the form, so be sure to read through it carefully. If your state is not listed above, you may want to check the most current version of your state's statutes or code, because your state legislature could adopt a form at any time.

Some states have specific living will provisions within a statutory health care power of attorney form (Arizona, Delaware, Georgia, Illinois, Nevada, New Hampshire, Oklahoma, Oregon, South Carolina, South Dakota, Tennessee, Utah, Vermont, Virginia, West Virginia, and Wisconsin). Still others just have spaces for you to write in any wishes you may have regarding life-prolonging procedures (California, District of Columbia, Idaho, Mississippi, New York, North Dakota, and Texas). A Connecticut health care power of attorney form appoints an agent to convey your wishes, but does not include any space for you to put your wishes in writing, so you need to be sure to tell your agent what you want or also execute a living will.

For states with no separate living will form, but with a living will provision within a power of attorney form, the entire state power of attorney/living will form has been included in Appendix B. If all you want is a living will, you can just complete the living will portions of the form and the section for signatures, witnesses, or notary. (If you want a health care power of attorney as well, you may want to see the *The Power of Attorney Handbook*, by Edward A. Haman. If you live in New York, see *New York Power of Attorney Handbook*, by William P. Coyle and Edward A. Haman. If you live in Florida, see *Florida Power of Attorney Handbook*, by Edward A. Haman. All three of these books are published by Sphinx Publishing and available through Sourcebooks, Inc.).

If you live in one of the states listed above as having a specific living will form, first refer to the listing for your state in Appendix A. Next, locate the form for your state in Appendix B. The specific state living will forms found in Appendix B, are basically as simple as Form 1 (discussed below), so the instructions given below for Form 1 will help you complete any of the state forms. Many of the state forms also have instructions on the forms themselves. All of them are simple to complete.

LIVING WILL
(FORM 1)

If you do not live in one of the states with its own living will form in Appendix B, you may use Form 1. To complete the Living Will (Form 1) you need to:

1. Type your name on the line in the first, unnumbered paragraph.

2. Read paragraphs 1, 2, and 3. Initial the line before the paragraph or paragraphs that agree with your wishes. Paragraph 1 concerns terminal illnesses or injuries, paragraph 2 concerns persistent vegetative states, and paragraph 3 concerns the situation where the burdens of treatment outweigh the expected benefits. If you *do* want life-prolonging procedures, you will initial paragraph 4 only. CAUTION: As to paragraphs 1 through 3, you may initial any *one* paragraph, two of these paragraphs, or all three of these

paragraphs. If you initial any of these three paragraphs, do not initial paragraph 4. If you initial paragraph 4, do not initial any of paragraphs 1 through 3. If you initial any of paragraphs 1 through 3, you must also initial the line before all of the medical treatments listed that you do *not* want. For most people, this will probably be all of them. There is also item "f" for you to fill in any other specific treatments you do not want.

3. Paragraph 5 provides space to type in any special instructions. You are not required to fill in anything here.

4. Fill in the date.

5. Type in your address where indicated below the signature line.

6. Take the form and your two witnesses to a notary public. Sign your name on the signature line, before two witnesses and a notary public. Also have the two witnesses sign (also before the notary) on the lines marked "Witness," and type in the witnesses' names and addresses below their signatures. (Not all states require a notary, but it won't hurt to have a notary attest to the signatures. This will also make the form appear more official to a doctor or hospital, and make them more likely to honor it.)

WITNESSES   Many states prohibit certain people from serving as a witness to your living will. Some of the state forms spellout who may or may not serve as a witness, so be sure to read the form carefully. Even if your state doesn't currently have any restrictions, it is still a good idea not to have a witness who is:

☞ Your spouse.

☞ Your parent.

☞ Your child.

☞ Related to you by blood, adoption, or marriage.

☞ Your physician or employed by your physician.

☞ A provider of health care to you, or an employee, agent, or patient of such a health care provider. This includes places such as hospitals and nursing homes, and their administrators, operators, and employees. It generally only applies to persons connected with a facility where you reside or which provides services to you. For example, if you have a friend who happens to work at a nursing home, but you are not a resident of that nursing home, that friend may act as your witness.

☞ Entitled to any part of your estate, either by law or through your will; or due to a claim against your estate.

☞ A beneficiary on your life insurance policy.

☞ Directly financially responsible for your medical care.

☞ Under the age of 18.

☞ The person named as your agent in a health care power of attorney.

NOTARIZED
SIGNATURES

Even if your state does not require a living will to be notarized, it is a good idea to have it notarized. This is just one more thing that may make it more likely for a health care provider to honor the living will without question. It will also be helpful if you are travelling to a state where living wills must be notarized. Form 45 is a notary page that you can attach to your living will (of course this will not be necessary if you are in a state with an approved form that already has a notary provision). CAUTION: Some states have specific requirements as to the form of a notarization statement (which can also be changed by the legislature at any time), so you should check with the notary you intend to use to be sure the form is valid.

USING YOUR LIVING WILL 5

Knowing what to do with a living will is just as important as having one.

EXAMPLE 1: Betty reads a magazine article telling her she needs a living will. So she has one prepared, stating that she does not want any artificial life-support provided if she is ever in a terminal condition, and signs it. Figuring that she should keep it with her other important papers, she puts it in her safe deposit box. Eight months later, Betty is in a serious car accident. She is brought to the hospital unconscious, and it quickly becomes obvious to the emergency room doctor that her injuries are so severe that she will never regain consciousness. She will die soon, unless she is hooked up to machines to keep her heart and lungs working. Her living will clearly states that she does not want to be hooked up to the machines, but since her living will is locked up in her safe deposit box, no one is aware of her wishes. Betty is hooked up to the machines with the permission of her daughter.

EXAMPLE 2: The situation is basically the same as above, except that Betty's living will states that she wants all efforts made to preserve her life. Betty lives in a state that allows spouse's or adult children to make this type of decision for a person who cannot communicate his or her desires. Again, her living will is locked in her safe deposit box, so no one knows her wishes. Betty's daughter tells the doctor not to hook Betty to the machines, believing this to be what Betty would want.

COPIES OF
YOUR LIVING
WILL

So, you see, it is important to let people know that you have a living will. For this reason, you should give copies to:

☞ Your spouse, adult children, or other close relatives or friends who may be contacted in the event you suffer a terminal illness or injury.

☞ Your regular, primary care doctor.

☞ Any specialist physician who is treating you.

☞ The local hospital where you are likely to be taken in an emergency.

☞ Any hospital, outpatient surgery center, or other health care facility where you will be receiving treatment.

☞ Any person you may have named as your agent in a health care power of attorney.

☞ Any nursing home or other type of assisted living facility in which you reside. This may also be required by state law.

You should also carry a copy with you when you travel.

LIVING WILLS
AND
EMERGENCY
MEDICAL CARE

There have been a few horror stories (which may just be rumor) of an emergency medical technician (EMT) refusing to provide emergency care to a person once it is learned the person has a living will. For purposes of emergency services, it is not necessary for the technician to know if the patient has a living will. If you are ever asked by an EMT if you have a living will, the safest response may be: "No." If asked if another person has a living will, the safest response may be: "Not that I know of." This should not be confused with a "do not resuscitate order," which is discussed in Chapter 6.

OTHER HEALTH CARE FORMS 6

DIRECTIVES FOR SPECIFIC MEDICAL PROCEDURES

A living will is generally executed well in advance of the need for medical procedures. However, when someone knows he or she will be going in the hospital for surgery, a specific form can be signed just for that particular hospital stay. Such a form can be more detailed and specific than a living will. Many hospitals have such forms for patients to complete prior to the procedure.

"DO NOT RESUSCITATE" ORDERS

A do not resuscitate order is a notation a physician makes on a patient's medical record. It informs the hospital staff that no resuscitation efforts are to be made in the event the patient's heart or breathing stops. This type of order may be abbreviated "DNR," and is also sometimes called a "no code order."

Traditionally a DNR order was issued by the attending physician when he or she believed that resuscitating the patient would do nothing but delay death and prolong pain. This was often done without the knowledge of the patient or the patient's family members. More recently, some states have passed laws giving family members rights to make decisions about DNR orders, and to allow a person to make an advance directive for a DNR order that is applicable to EMTs (this is different than an EMT refusing to treat because of the existence of a living will). Such laws are currently on the books in Alaska, Arizona, Arkansas, Colorado, Connecticut, Idaho, Maryland, Montana, New York, Rhode Island, South Carolina, Tennessee, Utah, Virginia, and West Virginia (see the listing for these states in Appendix A for more information).

REVOKING A LIVING WILL

If you execute a living will, then change your mind, there are two things you can do. First, you can execute a new living will that expresses your current desires. This would have the effect of cancelling your prior living will.

Second, you can simply revoke your living will, without making a new one. Most state laws provide that you may revoke your living will by simply telling your doctor. However, to be certain your doctor understands that you have changed your mind it would be better to put your revocation in writing. To do this, use the Revocation of Living Will (Form 2). To complete Form 2:

1. Type in your name and address on the first line in the main paragraph.

2. Type in the title of the living will you are revoking on the second line. This will be the title as it appears on the document, such as "Living Will," "Declaration," "Advance Directive," etc.

3. Type in the date of the living will you are revoking on the third line.

4. Type in the date on the line indicated, and sign on the signature line (sign before a notary if the living will you are revoking was also signed before a notary).

The living will form for Missouri (Form 23), contains a revocation provision. If you live in Missouri, you do not need to use Form 2 to revoke your Declaration, but can simply complete the revocation provision on Form 23.

STATEMENT OF DESIRES

In addition to a living will and a traditional will, you may want to have another document informing your family of certain things that you wish to have done. This can be accomplished with a Statement of Desires and Location of Property & Documents (Form 44). This is not a legally binding document, but merely a statement of your wishes, which you hope your family will follow.

In the event of death, many people have certain desires regarding the type of funeral and burial (or cremation, etc.), and other matters that cannot be taken care of in a will. A will may not be discovered until after burial, so it would do no good to include funeral and burial instructions in your will.

Another thing that can be done with such a document is to give your family members important information that will assist them in taking care of your estate. This includes such matters as:

☛ Where your will is located.

☛ A list of your assets. It is not always easy for the person handling your estate to find out everything that you own, especially things like stocks, bonds, and similar investments; and things stored somewhere other than at your home (such as a coin collection in a safe deposit box, a boat at a docking facility, a recreational vehicle in a storage lot, furniture at a self-storage company, etc.). Your list should include a detailed description of the item, and where it is located.

☛ A list of your life insurance policies, including the name, address, and telephone number of the insurance company (and of your insurance agent), and the policy number.

☛ A list of relatives, friends, and any other people you would like to be notified of your death. Include their names, addresses, and telephone numbers.

☛ Any desires you may have regarding the education and up-bringing of your minor children.

☛ Provisions for the custody and care of pets. You don't want your pets to go unfed while you are in the hospital, so be sure you discuss pet care with the relative or friend who will be notified in the event of an emergency. Your will should also state who you want to have your pets, and possibly include giving money to that person for food, veterinary care, etc.

☛ Instructions regarding your funeral. This should include information about any cemetery plot you may own, any pre-paid funeral plan, whether you want a traditional burial, burial at sea, cremation, etc., as well as any personal desires such as the type of music you want played. You may specify a lavish funeral, or state that you wish the least expensive burial in order to save assets for your heirs.

In order for such a document to be of any use, it must be in a place where it can easily be found by a family member. Therefore, it is not a good idea to put it in your safe deposit box. Once the bank finds out about your death it may seal your safe deposit box and only permit it to be opened with a court order. Because it takes time to obtain a court order, it may be well after the funeral that the contents of the safe deposit box become available.

APPENDIX A
STATE LAWS

This appendix lists each state alphabetically, and gives information about each state's laws concerning living wills. The following subjects are summarized for the applicable states:

THE LAW: This tells you where to find the law on living wills for your state. It will give the full title of the set of law books, with an example of how it is abbreviated. The symbol "§" means "section." Ask the librarian if you have any difficulty.

FORM(S): This will tell you which form, or forms, you will need from Appendix B of this book. First you will find the title of the form, followed by the form number. If your state has not adopted an official form, you will use Form 1, which will be the only form you need. If your state has adopted an official form, the name and number of that form will be given. You may also find a notation for optional forms. These are forms you may want to use in addition to the official form for the state. If your state's form does not have a provision for a notary public, Form 45 will be listed as an optional form. If your state's form may not clearly state your desires, Form 46 will be listed as an optional form. See pages 19, 20, and 30 for more discussion of the use of these optional forms.

TYPES OF CONDITIONS: This will tell you the various circumstances that are covered by each state's form. The most common types of situations covered by living wills are:

1. Terminal conditions. This is an illness or injury that is fairly certain to result in death. Many of the forms require death to be likely to occur "within a relatively short time," or some similar language. It is not certain what is meant by a relatively short time.

2. Persistent vegetative state. This may also be referred to as "permanently unconscious," "permanently comatose," "in a coma," etc. The idea is that the person is not aware of his or her surroundings, not able to communicate, and the condition is unlikely to change (the person's condition need not be terminal).

3. Where the burdens of treatment outweigh the benefits. This is where treatment will cause pain or discomfort, without appreciable benefits for the person or improvement of the condition (the person's condition need not be terminal).

DOCTOR CERTIFICATION: This will tell you if there are any requirements for a physician to officially certify the existence of the condition required for the living will to take effect. In some states, the person's doctor makes this determination informally. In other states, the physician must sign a written statement verifying the condition. In still other states there must be such a certificate signed by two or three physicians.

FOOD & WATER: This will tell you whether the state's form has any provisions regarding providing food and water to a patient by artificial means (i.e., by feeding tube through the mouth, nose, or intravenously). Some forms include this as a treatment to be withheld or withdrawn, others allow the person to choose whether this is to be included, and other forms don't say anything at all about this subject.

WITNESSES: This will tell you how many people need to witness your signature, and whether the signing needs to be notarized. As mentioned earlier in this book, it is a good idea to have signatures notarized, even if your state does not require it (see Chapter 4).

MISC.: This will give any other information that does not relate to one of the other categories. Most frequently noted will be other optional provisions in the form, and whether the form includes a pregnancy exception. Some state laws (and forms) provide that a living will may not be enforced if the person is pregnant. In such states, treatment is given to keep the person alive until the child can be born. Once the child is delivered, the living will goes back into effect and further treatment can be stopped.

These notes will mention where possible problems may arise.

In the section on THE LAW it will also be noted if the state has any provisions for health care powers of attorney, although such forms are beyond the scope of this book. For more information about how you can prepare your own health care power of attorney, or financial power of attorney, see *The Power of Attorney Handbook*, by Edward A. Haman (in Florida, see

Florida Power of Attorney Handbook, by Edward A. Haman; in New York, see *New York Power of Attorney Handbook*, by William P. Coyle and Edward A. Haman). All three of these books are published by Sourcebooks, Inc/Sphinx.

ALABAMA

THE LAW: "Natural Death Act," Code of Alabama, Title 22, Chapter 8A, Section 22-8A-1 (C.A. §22-8A-1). Form at C.A. §22-8A-4. Look for volume 14.

FORM(S): DECLARATION (Form 3). Optional: Forms 45 and 46.

TYPES OF CONDITIONS: Applies to terminal condition.

DOCTOR CERTIFICATION: 2 physicians, one of whom is the attending physician.

FOOD & WATER: No provision.

WITNESSES: 2 witnesses; no notary.

ALASKA

THE LAW: Alaska Statutes, Title 18, Chapter 12, Section 18.12.010 (A.S. §18.12.010), titled "Living Wills and Do Not Resuscitate Orders." Form at A.S. §18.12.010(c). DNR: A.S. §18.12.035. Look for volume 5.

FORM(S): DECLARATION (Form 4). Sign before a notary, although this is optional. Optional: Form 46.

TYPES OF CONDITIONS: Applies to an "incurable or irreversible condition" that will cause death "within a relatively short time."

DOCTOR CERTIFICATION: Attending physician must certify in person's medical record.

FOOD & WATER: Has optional provision.

WITNESSES: 2 witnesses OR notary.

MISC.: Cards, necklaces, bracelets, etc., identifying a person as having a living will or do not resuscitate order are available from the Department of Health and Social Services.

ARIZONA

THE LAW: Living will form is part of a health care power of attorney, Arizona Revised Statutes, Section 36-3262 (A.R.S. §36-3262). Form at A.R.S. §36-3224. (There is also a "Prehospital Medical Care Directive," A.R.S. §36-3251.) DNR: A.R.S. §36-32-51.

FORM(S): HEALTH CARE POWER OF ATTORNEY (Form 5). You will note that this is a form which also include provisions for a health care power of attorney, autopsy, organ donation, and a physician affidavit (verifying that he or she has discussed treatment options and the probable consequences, and agrees to comply with your wishes as expressed in the power of attorney and living will). This form also has an optional provision for a pregnancy exception. Part 5 is the living will portion of this form. If you only want a living will, then only complete Part 5 and the signature/witness/notary sections. Optional: Form 46.

TYPES OF CONDITIONS: Has options for living will to cover terminal condition; or irreversible coma, and persistent vegetative state that doctor believes to be irreversible or incurable.

DOCTOR CERTIFICATION: Not required.

FOOD & WATER: Has optional provision.

WITNESSES: 2 witnesses OR notary.

ARKANSAS

THE LAW: "Arkansas Rights of the Terminally Ill or Permanently Unconscious Act," Arkansas Code of 1987 Annotated, Title 20, Chapter 17, Section 20-17-201 (A.C.A. §20-17-201). Form at A.C.A. §20-17-202. Look for volume 20A. DNR: A.C.A. §20-13-901 to 908.

FORM(S): DECLARATION (Form 6). In both main paragraphs, you must cross out one of the two statements in brackets "[   ]", whichever does *not* express your wishes. One is a statement that you want treatment withheld or withdrawn; the other appoints a person ("health care proxy") to provide instructions. If you cross out the first option, you will need to fill in the name of the person you want as your health care proxy. Optional: Forms 45 and 46.

TYPES OF CONDITIONS: Applies to an "incurable or irreversible condition" that will cause death "within a relatively short time"; and to being "permanently unconscious."

[Arkansas listing continues on the next page.]

DOCTOR CERTIFICATION: Not required.

FOOD & WATER: No provision.

WITNESSES: 2 witnesses; no notary.

CALIFORNIA

THE LAW: No specific provisions for living wills. [Health care power of attorney provisions found in *West's* Annotated California Codes, Probate Code, Section 4700 et seq. (A.C.P.C. §4700 et seq.), titled "Durable Power of Attorney for Health Care." Health care power of attorney form found in 1997 Cumulative Pocket Part at A.C.P.C. §4771.]

FORM(S): LIVING WILL (Form 1).

COLORADO

THE LAW: "Colorado Medical Treatment Decisions Act," *West's* Colorado Revised Statutes Annotated, Title 15, Article 18, Section 15-18-101 (C.R.S.A. §15-18-101). Form at C.R.S.A. §15-18-104 (in 1996 Supplement Pamphlet). DNR: C.R.S.A. §15-18.6-101 to 108 (called "CPR directive").

FORM(S): DECLARATION AS TO MEDICAL OR SURGICAL TREATMENT (Form 7). Optional: Form 46.

TYPES OF CONDITIONS: Applies if there is a terminal condition that is incurable of irreversible; or if "unconscious, comatose, or otherwise incompetent so as to be unable to make or communicate responsible decisions" for seven or more days. As written, it does not appear that a terminal condition is required to qualify under the provision for being unconscious, comatose or incompetent for at least seven days.

DOCTOR CERTIFICATION: 2 physicians must certify to the condition being terminal; but not to being unconscious, comatose or otherwise incompetent.

FOOD & WATER: Has various options.

WITNESSES: 2 witnesses AND notary for signer and witnesses

CONNECTICUT

THE LAW: Connecticut General Statutes Annotated, Title 19a, Section 19a-570 (C.G.S.A. §19a-570), titled "Removal of Life Support Systems." Look for volume 11. Form at C.G.S.A. §19a-575 in the 1997 Cumulative Annual Pocket Part. DNR: C.G.S.A. §19a-580d. (Health care power of attorney form at C.G.S.A. §§ 19a-575a and 19a-577.)

FORM(S): DOCUMENT CONCERNING WITHHOLDING OR WITHDRAWAL OF LIFE SUPPORT SYSTEMS (Form 8). Optional: Forms 45 and 46.

TYPES OF CONDITIONS: Applies if there is a terminal condition or person is "permanently unconscious."

DOCTOR CERTIFICATION: Not required.

FOOD & WATER: Optional provisions (included as being withdrawn or withheld unless you cross it out and initial it).

WITNESSES: 2 witnesses; no notary.

DELAWARE

THE LAW: Delaware Code Annotated, Title 16, Section 2501 (D.C.A. 16 §2501), titled "Health-Care Decisions." Living will form is Part 2 of the statutory health care power of attorney at D.C.A. §2505. Look for volume 9.

FORM(S): ADVANCE HEALTH-CARE DIRECTIVE (Form 9). You will note that this is a form which also includes provisions for a health care power of attorney, anatomical gifts, and designating a primary physician. Part 2 is the living will portion of this form. If you only want a living will, then only complete Part 2 and the signature/witness/notary sections. Optional: Forms 45 and 46.

TYPES OF CONDITIONS: Applies to terminal conditions and where person is "permanently unconscious."

DOCTOR CERTIFICATION: Not required.

FOOD & WATER: Optional provisions.

WITNESSES: 2 witnesses; no notary.

DISTRICT OF COLUMBIA

THE LAW: No specific provisions for living wills. [Health care power of attorney provisions found in District of Columbia Code, Title 21, Section 2201 (D.C.C. §21-2201), titled "Health-Care Decisions." The books have "D.C. Code" on the spine, and "District of Columbia Code" on the front cover. Look for volume 5. Health care power of attorney form at D.C.C. §21-2207.]

FORM(S): LIVING WILL (Form 1).

FLORIDA

THE LAW: Florida Statutes, Chapter 765, Section 765.301 (F.S. §765.301). Living will form at F.S. §765.303. [Health Care Surrogate (i.e., health care power of attorney) form found at F.S. §765.203. See *Florida Power of Attorney Handbook*, by Edward A. Haman (Sphinx Publishing/Sourcebooks, Inc.), for more detailed information on the health care power of attorney.] There are also provisions for family members to make decisions in the absence of a living will or health care power of attorney, F.S. §765.401.

FORM(S): LIVING WILL (Form 10). Optional: Forms 45 and 46.

TYPES OF CONDITIONS: Applies to a terminal condition with "no medical probability" of recovery.

DOCTOR CERTIFICATION: 2 physicians, one of whom is the "attending or treating" physician.

FOOD & WATER: No provision.

WITNESSES: 2 witnesses; no notary.

MISC.: Has space to designate a "surrogate" to carry out desires as expressed (i.e., give consent to terminate or withhold treatment).

GEORGIA

THE LAW: No specific provisions for living wills. [Health care power of attorney provisions found in the "Durable Power of Attorney for Health Care Act," Official Code of Georgia Annotated, Title 31, Chapter 36, Section 31-36-1 (O.C.G.A. §31-36-1). Volume 23. Health care power of attorney form at O.C.G.A. §31-26-10.]

FORM(S): LIVING WILL (Form 1).

HAWAII

THE LAW: Hawaii Revised Statutes, Section 327D-4 (H.R.S. §327D-4). A physician's form for certifying disability at H.R.S. §327D-10, in 1993 Cumulative Supplement. [Health care power of attorney is provided for in the "Uniform Durable Power of Attorney Act" (H.R.S. §551D-1). Power of attorney form at H.R.S. §551D-2.6.]

FORM(S): DECLARATION (Form 11). Optional: Form 46.

TYPES OF CONDITIONS: Applies to a terminal condition or the "permanent loss of the ability to communicate concerning medical treatment decisions."

DOCTOR CERTIFICATION: Not required.

FOOD & WATER: Has optional provisions.

WITNESSES: 2 witnesses AND notary.

IDAHO

THE LAW: "Natural Death Act," Idaho Code, Title 39, Chapter 45, Section 39-4501 (I.C. §39-4501). Living will form at I.C. §39-4504. [Health care powers of attorney are covered in the I.C. §39-4501; form at I.C. §39-4505.] Look for volume 7A. DNR: I.C. §39-151 to 165 in 1996 Cumulative Pocket Supplement.

FORM(S): A LIVING WILL (Form 12). Optional: Forms 45 and 46.

TYPES OF CONDITIONS: Applies to a terminal condition or being in a "persistent vegetative state."

[Idaho listing continues on the next page.]

DOCTOR CERTIFICATION: 2 "medical doctors."

FOOD & WATER: Has optional provisions.

WITNESSES: 2 witnesses; no notary.

MISC.: Has space to designate proxy to make health care decisions, but this paragraph also states "I have duly executed a Durable Power of Attorney for health care decisions on this date." Has pregnancy exception.

ILLINOIS

THE LAW: "Illinois Living Will Act," *West's* Smith Hurd Illinois Compiled Statutes Annotated, Chapter 755, Section 35/1 (755 ILCS 35/1). Illinois has two sets of statutes, with different numbering systems. One is "Smith-Hurd Illinois Annotated Statutes," (abbreviated "I.A.S."), and the other is "*West's* Smith Hurd Illinois Compiled Statutes Annotated," (abbreviated "ILCS"). References are given to both sets. (Health care power of attorney covered in "Health Care Surrogate Act," 110 1/2 I.A.S. §804-1; and 755 ILCS 45/4-1. Health care power of attorney form at 110 1/2 I.A.S. §804-10; and 755 ILCS 45/4-10.)

FORM(S): DECLARATION (Form 13). Optional: Forms 45 and 46.

TYPES OF CONDITIONS: Applies to terminal conditions.

DOCTOR CERTIFICATION: Not required.

FOOD & WATER: No provisions.

WITNESSES: 2 witnesses; no notary.

INDIANA

THE LAW: *West's* Annotated Indiana Code, Title 16, Article 35, Chapter 4, Section 16-36-4-1 (A.I.C. §16-36-4-1). Indiana has two forms, one for refusing treatment and one for requesting treatment. Form for refusing life-prolonging procedures at A.I.C. §16-36-4-10. Form for requesting life-prolonging procedures at A.I.C. §16-36-4-11. (Information about health care powers of attorney found at A.I.C. §16-36-1-1, titled "Health Care Consent," which allows appointment of a "health care representative," but no form is provided. This can also be accomplished with a general power of attorney pursuant to A.I.C. §30-5-5-1, which includes a provision for health care powers.) Living will and health care power of attorney provisions are found in a separate paperback volume entitled "1995 Supplementary Pamphlet."

FORM(S): LIVING WILL DECLARATION (Form 14), if you do **not** want life-prolonging procedures. Optional: Forms 45 and 46. LIFE PROLONGING PROCEDURES DECLARATION (Form 15) if you **want** life-prolonging procedures. Optional: Forms 45.

TYPES OF CONDITIONS: Form for refusing treatment applies to a terminal condition where "death will occur within a short time."

DOCTOR CERTIFICATION: Refusal of treatment requires certification by the attending physician.

FOOD & WATER: Refusal of treatment still requires the provision of food and water (i.e., there is no option on the form to refuse food and water).

WITNESSES: 2 witnesses; no notary.

IOWA

THE LAW: Living wills provided for in Iowa Code Annotated, Section 144A.1 (I.C.A. §144A.1); form at I.C.A. §144A.3. Look in the 1997 Cumulative Annual Pocket Part to volume 9. (Health care power of attorney form at I.C.A. §144B.5.)

FORM(S): LIVING WILL (Form 16). Optional: Forms 45 and 46.

TYPES OF CONDITIONS: Applies to terminal condition and being in a "state of permanent unconsciousness."

DOCTOR CERTIFICATION: Not required.

[Iowa listing continues on the next page.]

FOOD & WATER: No provisions.

WITNESSES: 2 witnesses; no notary.

KANSAS

THE LAW: No specific provisions for living wills. [Health care power of attorney provisions found in Kansas Statutes Annotated, Section 58-625 (K.S.A. §58-625). Form for health care power of attorney at K.S.A. §58-632.] You may find these volumes as either "*Vernon's* Kansas Statutes Annotated," or "Kansas Statutes Annotated, Official." The supplement is a pocket part in "Vernon's" and a separate soft-cover volume in the "Official." Both sets have very poor indexing systems.

FORM(S): LIVING WILL (Form 1).

KENTUCKY

THE LAW: "Kentucky Living Will Directive Act," Kentucky Revised Statutes, Chapter 311, Section 311.620 (K.R.S. §311.620). Form at K.R.S. §311.625.

FORM(S): Living Will Directive (Form 17). Optional: Form 46.

TYPES OF CONDITIONS: Applies to terminal condition or if person is "permanently unconscious."

DOCTOR CERTIFICATION: Not required.

FOOD & WATER: Optional provisions.

WITNESSES: 2 witnesses OR notary.

MISC.: Has pregnancy exception.

LOUISIANA

THE LAW: "Natural Death Act," *West's* Louisiana Statutes Annotated, Revised Statutes, Section 40.1299.58.1 (LSA Revised Statutes §40:1299.58.1). Living will form at LSA Revised Statutes §40:1299.58.3 (Volume 22C). The *West's* Louisiana Statutes Annotated set is divided into topics, such as "Civil Code," "Revised Statutes," etc., so be sure you have the volumes titled "Revised Statutes." The books have "*West's* LSA Revised Statutes" on the spine, and "*West's* Louisiana Revised Statutes" on the front cover. You may also designate a living will on your Louisiana driver's license according to LSA Revised Statutes §32:410.

FORM(S): DECLARATION (Form 18). Optional: Forms 45 and 46.

TYPES OF CONDITIONS: This statutory form has many problems. Read the second paragraph of Form 18 carefully (this paragraph begins with the words "If at any time"). In an apparent attempt to make it comprehensive, the legislature has drafted a document that contains so much verbiage that it isn't clear what it means. Many questions arise. For example, does the comatose state need to be accompanied by a terminal condition? If so, why even mention comatose states? Or, the form also states that death must "occur whether or not life-sustaining procedures are utilized." This goes against a central purpose of a living will, which is to avoid situations where life is maintained indefinitely by life-sustaining procedures.

DOCTOR CERTIFICATION: Certification by 2 physicians, one of whom is the attending physician.

FOOD & WATER: No provision.

WITNESSES: 2 witnesses; no notary.

MAINE

THE LAW: Living will is part of a health care power of attorney. Maine Revised Statutes Annotated, Title 18-A, Section 5-801 (18-A M.R.S.A. §5-801). "Uniform Rights of the Terminally Ill Act." Form at 18-A M.R.S.A. §5-804. Health care power of attorney is also provided for in 18-A M.R.S.A. §5-506, but no form in that statute.

FORM(S): ADVANCE HEALTH-CARE DIRECTIVE (Form 19). You will note that this is a form which also includes provisions for a health care power of attorney, organ donation, and
[Maine listing is continued on the next page.]

designating a primary physician. This form also has an optional provision for a pregnancy exception. Part 2 is the living will portion of this form. If you only want a living will, then only complete Part 2 and the signature/witness/notary sections. Optional: Forms 45 and 46.

TYPES OF CONDITIONS: Applies to (1) an incurable and irreversible condition that will result in death within a relatively short time, (2) unconsciousness with a reasonable degree of medical certainty that consciousness will not be regained, and (3) where the likely risks and burdens of treatment outweigh the expected benefits.

DOCTOR CERTIFICATION: Not required.

FOOD & WATER: Optional provisions.

WITNESSES: Optional provision for 2 witnesses; no notary.

MARYLAND

THE LAW: Annotated Code of Maryland, Health-General, Section 5-601 (A.C.M., HG §5-601). Living will and health care power of attorney forms at A.C.M., HG §5-603). These volumes are arranged by subject, so be sure you have the volume marked "Health-General." Advance directive for DNR: A.C.M., HG §5-608.

FORM(S): HEALTH CARE DECISION MAKING FORMS (Form 20). Optional: Forms 45 and 46.

TYPES OF CONDITIONS: Applies in the case of a terminal condition, and a persistent vegetative state with no expectation of recovery "within a medically appropriate period."

DOCTOR CERTIFICATION: Not required.

FOOD & WATER: Optional provisions.

WITNESSES: 2 witnesses; no notary.

MISC.: Space is provided to fill in any instructions to be followed in the event a female signer is pregnant.

MASSACHUSETTS

THE LAW: No specific provisions for living wills. [Health care powers of attorney are discussed in Annotated Laws of Massachusetts, Chapter 201D, Section 1 (A.L.M., C. 201D, §1). Health care power of attorney form may be found at A.L.M. Ch. 201D, §4.]

FORM(S): LIVING WILL (Form 1).

MICHIGAN

THE LAW: No specific provisions for living wills. The index listing for living wills refers you to the provision titled "Designation of patient advocate," which authorizes such a designation, but does not provide a form for either a living will or a health care power of attorney. M.S.A. §27.5496; M.C.L.A. §700.496. Michigan has two official sets of laws, each from a different publisher. One is Michigan Statutes Annotated, (abbreviated M.S.A.). and the other is Michigan Compiled Laws Annotated, (abbreviated M.C.L.A.). Each has a completely different numbering system. References are given to both sets as most libraries will only have one set. Ignore the volume and chapter numbers, and look for section numbers.

FORM(S): LIVING WILL (Form 1).

MINNESOTA

THE LAW: "Minnesota Living Will Act," Minnesota Statutes Annotated, Section 145B.01 (M.S.A. §145B.01). Living will form at M.S.A. §145B.04. Look for volume 11, 1996 Supplemental Pamphlet. Living will can also be noted on a driver's license, M.S.A. §171.07. (Health care power of attorney may be found at M.S.A. §145C.01, titled "Durable Power of Attorney for Health Care." Health care power of attorney form found at M.S.A. §145C.05.)

FORM(S): HEALTH CARE LIVING WILL (Form 21). This is not a "check-the-box" type of form, or one which takes a certain position on various issues. You will need to fill in your wishes for each numbered paragraph. These include topics such as treatment options, food and water, organ donation, and designating a proxy and an alternate proxy. Optional: Form 46.

[Minnesota listing continues on the next page.]

TYPES OF CONDITIONS: Applies to a terminal condition, but also has a space to fill in specific circumstances.

DOCTOR CERTIFICATION: Not required.

FOOD & WATER: Optional provisions.

WITNESSES: Notary OR 2 witnesses.

MISSISSIPPI

THE LAW: Mississippi Code 1972 Annotated, Title 41, Section 41-41-101 (M.C. §41-41-101), titled "Withdrawal of Life-Saving Mechanism." Living will form at M.C. §41-41-107. Revocation form at M.C. §41-41-109. (Health care powers of attorney are provided for in the "Durable Power of Attorney for Health Care Act," M.C. §41-41-151, with forms at §§41-41-159 and 41-41-163.) If not found in the regular volume, look for the Cumulative Supplement to volume 11 (this is a separate book from the regular volume 11).

FORM(S): DECLARATION (Form 22). Optional: Forms 45 and 46.

TYPES OF CONDITIONS: Applies if there is a "terminal condition," causing "severe distress or unconsciousness," and death is "imminent."

DOCTOR CERTIFICATION: 3 physicians, one of whom is the attending physician.

FOOD & WATER: No provision.

WITNESSES: 2 witnesses; no notary.

MISC.: Has pregnancy exception. Living will must be filed with the Bureau of Vital Statistics, Mississippi State Board of Health.

MISSOURI

THE LAW: *Vernon's* Annotated Missouri Statutes, Chapter 459, Section 459.010 (A.M.S. §459.010). Living will form at A.M.S. §459.015. Volume 25. (Health care powers of attorney provided for in the "Durable Power of Attorney for Health Care Act," A.M.S. §404.800. Volume 21, 1996 Cumulative Annual Pocket Part. No health care power of attorney form provided.)

FORM(S): DECLARATION (Form 23). Optional: Forms 45 and 46.

TYPES OF CONDITIONS: Applies to terminal conditions.

DOCTOR CERTIFICATION: Not required.

FOOD & WATER: No provision.

WITNESSES: 2 witnesses; no notary.

MISC.: Form has revocation provision.

MONTANA

THE LAW: Montana Code Annotated, Title 50, Chapter 9, Section 50-9-103 (M.C.A. §50-9-103). Look for volume 8. DNR: M.C.A. §50-10-101 to 107. The Montana Code is in paperback volumes, with the annotations in a separate set of binders.

FORM(S): Directive to Physicians (Form 24). Optional: Forms 45 and 46.

TYPES OF CONDITIONS: Applies to an "incurable or irreversible condition" that will cause death "within a relatively short time."

DOCTOR CERTIFICATION: Not required, however the form does state that it is to be the attending physician's opinion that the conditions are met.

FOOD & WATER: No provision.

WITNESSES: 2 witnesses; no notary.

NEBRASKA

THE LAW: "Rights of the Terminally Ill Act," Revised Statutes of Nebraska, Chapter 20, Section 20-401 (R.S.A. §20-401). Living will form at R.S.N. §20-204. Look in 1996 Cumulative Supplement, Volume 1. (Heath care power of attorney provided for in R.S.N. §30-3401, titled "Health Care Power of Attorney," with form at R.S.N. §30-3408. Look for volume 2A.)

FORM(S): DECLARATION (Form 25). Optional: Form 46.

TYPES OF CONDITIONS: Applies to terminal condition or "persistent vegetative state."

DOCTOR CERTIFICATION: Not required.

FOOD & WATER: No provision.

WITNESSES: 2 witnesses OR notary.

NEVADA

THE LAW: Nevada Revised Statutes Annotated, Chapter 449, Section 449:610 (N.R.S.A.§449:610). Form for living will at N.R.S.A. §449.610. [Health care power of attorney form at N.R.S.A. §449.613. Also see N.R.S.A. §449.830. This is a part of the health care power of attorney. Look for the 1995 Cumulative Supplement to volume 12 (this is a separate book).]

FORM(S): DIRECTIVE REGARDING HEALTH CARE DECISIONS (Form 26). Optional: Form 46.

TYPES OF CONDITIONS: Applies to (1) irreversible coma, (2) incurable or terminal condition or illness, with no reasonable hope of long term recovery or survival, or (3) the burdens of treatment outweigh the expected benefits.

DOCTOR CERTIFICATION: Not required.

FOOD & WATER: Optional provision.

WITNESSES: 2 witnesses OR notary. One of the witnesses must sign in two places.

NEW HAMPSHIRE

THE LAW: New Hampshire Revised Statutes Annotated 1992, Chapter 137-H, Section 137-H:1 (N.H.R.S.A. §137-H:1). Ignore "title" numbers; look for "chapter" numbers. Living will form at N.H.R.S.A. §137-H:3. (Health care powers of attorney covered at N.H.R.S.A. §137-J:1, with form at N.H.R.S.A. §137-J:15.)

FORM(S): DECLARATION (Form 27). Optional: Form 46.

TYPES OF CONDITIONS: Applies to a "terminal" or "permanently unconscious" condition.

DOCTOR CERTIFICATION: Two physicians.

FOOD & WATER: Optional provision.

WITNESSES: 2 witnesses AND notary of signer and witnesses.

NEW JERSEY

THE LAW: "New Jersey Advance Directives for Health Care Act," NJSA (for New Jersey Statutes Annotated), Title 26, Section 26H-53. Authorizes both a "proxy directive" and an "instructional directive," but does not provide any forms.

FORM(S): LIVING WILL (Form 1).

TYPES OF CONDITIONS: Applies to a "terminal" or "permanently unconscious" condition.

DOCTOR CERTIFICATION: Attending physician and another must certify person lacks decision making capacity, and this must be noted in the person's medical record. If incapacity is due to a mental or psychological condition, one of the certifications must be by "a physician with appropriate special training or experience."

WITNESSES: 2 witnesses OR signature before notary, attorney at law, or other person authorized to administer oaths.

NEW MEXICO

THE LAW: New Mexico Statutes 1978 Annotated, Chapter 24, Section 24-7A-1 (N.M.S.A. §24-7A-1), titled "Uniform Health-Care Decisions." Look for volume 5. Living will is Part 2 of the health care power of attorney form, and is titled "Instructions for Health Care." Health care power of attorney form at N.M.S.A. §24-7A-4. A supplement to the Statutes is found at the end of each chapter.

FORM(S): OPTIONAL ADVANCE HEALTH-CARE DIRECTIVE (Form 28). You will note that this is a form which also includes provisions for a health care power of attorney, and designating a primary physician. Part 2 is the living will portion of this form. If you only want a living will, then only complete Part 2 and the signature/witness/notary sections. Optional: Forms 45 and 46.

TYPES OF CONDITIONS: Applies to (1) terminal condition, (2) being permanently unconscious, and (3) where "the likely risks and burdens of treatment would outweigh the expected benefits."

DOCTOR CERTIFICATION: The "physician in charge" and one other physician must certify in writing to the terminal condition or irreversible coma, with a copy placed in the person's medical record.

FOOD & WATER: Optional provisions.

WITNESSES: Statutes states it must be executed in the same manner as a will, and the official form just requires signature (and has spaces for 2 witnesses designated as "Optional").

MISC.: Has optional provision to request all possible procedures.

NEW YORK

THE LAW: No specific provisions for living wills. [*McKinney's* Consolidated Laws of New York Annotated, Public Health §2980 (C.L.N.Y., Public Health §2980), called "Health Care Agents and Proxies." This section relates to health care powers of attorney, with form called "Health Care Proxy" found at §2981(d).] Advance directive for DNR: C.L.N.Y., Public Health §2977. This set of books is divided according to subject, so be sure you have the volume marked "Public Health."

FORM(S): LIVING WILL (Form 1).

NORTH CAROLINA

THE LAW: Living will provisions at General Statutes of North Carolina, Chapter 90, Section 90-307 (G.S.N.C. §90-307), titled "Right to Natural Death; Brain Death." Living will form at G.S.N.C. §90-321(d). (Health care power of attorney at G.S.N.C. §32A-15, titled "Health Care Powers of Attorney." Form at G.S.N.C. §32A-25.)

FORM(S): **Declaration Of A Desire For A Natural Death** (Form29). Optional: Form 46.

TYPES OF CONDITIONS: Applies to terminal condition or if "in a persistent vegetative state."

DOCTOR CERTIFICATION: Not required.

FOOD & WATER: Optional provisions.

WITNESSES: 2 witnesses AND acknowledgment of notary, court clerk, or assistant court clerk of signatures of the signer and witnesses.

NORTH DAKOTA

THE LAW: No specific provisions for living wills. [Health care power of attorney found at North Dakota Century Code Annotated, Title 23, Chapter 06.5, Section 23-06.5-1 (N.D.C.C. §23-06.5-1), titled "Durable Power of Attorney for Health Care." Health care power of attorney form at N.D.C.C. §23-06.5-17. Look for volume 4A, 1995 Pocket Supplement.]

FORM(S): LIVING WILL (Form 1)

OHIO

THE LAW: No specific provision for living wills. [Health care power of attorney at *Page's* Ohio Revised Code Annotated, Section 1337.11 (O.R.S. §1337.11, but no form is provided. Also see O.R.S. §2133.01, titled "Modified Uniform Rights of the Terminally Ill Act."]

FORM(S): LIVING WILL (Form 1).

OKLAHOMA

THE LAW: Living will is part of health care power of attorney form. Oklahoma Statutes Annotated, Title 63, Section 3101 (63 O.S.A. §3101), titled "Oklahoma Rights of the Terminally Ill or Persistently Unconscious Act." Health care power of attorney form found at 63 O.S.A. §3101.4. Look for 1996 Cumulative Annual Pocket Part.

FORM(S): **Advance Directive for Health Care** (Form 30). You will note that this is a form which also includes provisions for a health care power of attorney ("proxy"), and anatomical gifts. This form also has an optional provision for a pregnancy exception. Part I is the living will portion of this form. If you only want a living will, then only complete Part I and the signature/witness/notary sections. Optional: Forms 45 and 46.

TYPES OF CONDITIONS: Applies to a terminal condition or when the person is persistently unconscious. For terminal conditions, it must be determined that death will result within six months.

DOCTOR CERTIFICATION: 2 physicians.

FOOD & WATER: Optional provision.

WITNESSES: 2 witnesses; no notary

OREGON

THE LAW: Living will is a part of the health care power of attorney form. Oregon Revised Statutes Annotated, Chapter 127, Section 127.505 (O.R.S. §127.505). Health care power of attorney form at O.R.S. §127.530.

FORM(S): ADVANCE DIRECTIVE (Form 31). You will note that this is a form which also includes provisions for a health care power of attorney ("health care representative"). If you only want a living will, then only complete Part C and the signature/witness/notary sections. Optional: Forms 45 and 46.

TYPES OF CONDITIONS: Applies if the person (1) is close to death and life support would only postpone the moment of death, (2) is permanently unconscious, or (3) has an advanced progressive illness (as described in the form); or (4) if life support would cause "permanent and severe pain" and would not help the person's condition.

DOCTOR CERTIFICATION: Not required.

FOOD & WATER: Optional provisions.

WITNESSES: 2 witnesses; no notary.

PENNSYLVANIA

THE LAW: No specific provision for living wills. [Health care power of attorney found in the "Advance Directive for Health Care Act," *Purdon's* Pennsylvania Consolidated Statutes Annotated, Title 20, Section 20-5401 (20 Pa.C.S.A. §5401). Health care power of attorney form at 20 Pa.C.S.A. §5404.]

FORM(S): LIVING WILL (Form 1).

RHODE ISLAND

THE LAW: "Rights of the Terminally Ill Act," General Laws of Rhode Island, Section 23-4.11-1 (G.L.R.I. §23-4.11-1). [Health care power of attorney found in the "Health Care Power of Attorney Act," General Laws of Rhode Island, Section 23-4.10-1 (G.L.R.I. §23-4.10-1). Health care power of attorney form at G.L.R.I. §23-4.11-3.] DNR: G.L.R.I. §23-4.11-14. Look for volume 4B. Ignore "Title" and "Chapter" numbers.

FORM(S): DECLARATION (Form 32). Optional: Forms 45 and 46.

TYPES OF CONDITIONS: Applies if the person has an "incurable or irreversible condition" that will cause death "within a relatively short time."

DOCTOR CERTIFICATION: Not required.

FOOD & WATER: Optional provision.

WITNESSES: 2 witnesses; no notary.

SOUTH CAROLINA

THE LAW: "Death With Dignity Act," Code of Laws of South Carolina, Title 44, Section 44-77-10 (C.L.S.C. §44-77-10). (Health care power of attorney form at §44-77-50. "Adult Health Care Consent Act," at C.L.S.C. §44-66-10, discusses consent for medical treatment and states that this subject can be included in a durable power of attorney, but no form is provided.) DNR: C.L.S.C. §44-78-10 to 65.

FORM(S): DECLARATION OF A DESIRE FOR A NATURAL DEATH (Form 33). The form states several optional revocation procedures. Also includes option to appoint an agent for the purpose of enforcing or revoking the living will. Optional: Form 46.

TYPES OF CONDITIONS: Applies to terminal conditions or permanent unconsciousness.

DOCTOR CERTIFICATION: 2 physicians.

FOOD & WATER: Optional provisions.

WITNESSES: 2 witnesses AND notary of signer and witnesses.

SOUTH DAKOTA

THE LAW: South Dakota Codified Laws, Title 34, Section 34-12D-1 (S.D.C.L §34-12D-1), titled "Living Wills." Look for 1993 Pocket Supplement to volume 11A. (Health care provisions are also authorized by S.D.C.L. §§59-7-2.5 and 34-12C-3, but no forms.)

FORM(S): LIVING WILL DECLARATION (Form 34). Optional: Form 46.

TYPES OF CONDITIONS: Applies to terminal conditions.

DOCTOR CERTIFICATION: Not required.

FOOD & WATER: Optional provisions.

WITNESSES: 2 witnesses AND notary of signer and witnesses.

TENNESSEE

THE LAW: Tennessee Code Annotated, Title 34, Section 34-6-203 (T.C.A. §34-6-203). DNR: T.C.A. §68-140-601.

FORM(S): LIVING WILL (Form 35). Optional: Form46.

TYPES OF CONDITIONS: Applies to terminal conditions.

DOCTOR CERTIFICATION: Not required.

FOOD & WATER: Optional provisions.

WITNESSES: 2 witnesses AND notary of signer and witnesses.

MISC.: Also has option for organ donations.

TEXAS

THE LAW: "Natural Death Act," *Vernon's* Texas Codes Annotated, Health and Safety, Section 672.001 (T.C.A., Health and Safety Code §672.001) Living will form at T.C.A, Health and Safety Code §672.004. (Health care power of attorney form at T.C.A., Health and Safety §672.004. Also see T.C.A., Civil Practice & Remedies §135.001.) The T.C.A. is divided into subjects, so be sure you have the proper subject volume. Also, be sure you have the volumes marked "*Vernon's* Texas Codes Annotated;" not those marked "*Vernon's* Texas Civil Statutes," which have a volume marked "Health."

FORM(S): DIRECTIVE TO PHYSICIANS (Form 36). Optional: Forms 45 and 46.

TYPES OF CONDITIONS: Applies to terminal conditions.

DOCTOR CERTIFICATION: 2 physicians must certify condition is terminal; and attending physician must determine "death is imminent or will result within a relatively short time without the application of life-sustaining procedures."

FOOD & WATER: No provision.

WITNESSES: 2 witnesses; no notary.

MISC.: Has pregnancy limitation.

UTAH

THE LAW: Utah Code Annotated 1953, Title 75, Chapter 2, Section 75-2-1104 (U.C.A. §75-2-1104). DNR: U.C.A. §75-2-1105.5. Look in the Supplement to volume 8A if not found in the main volume.

FORM(S): DIRECTIVE TO PHYSICIANS AND PROVIDERS OF MEDICAL SERVICES (Form 3). Optional: Forms 45 and 46.

TYPES OF CONDITIONS: Applies to terminal condition or persistent vegetative state.

DOCTOR CERTIFICATION: 2 physicians.

FOOD & WATER: Provides that food and water *will* be withheld (no option to designate otherwise, unless you cross out this provision).

WITNESSES: 2 witnesses; no notary.

VERMONT

THE LAW: Vermont Statutes Annotated, Title 18, Section 5252 (18 V.S.A. §5252). Ignore "Chapter" numbers. Living will is referred to as a "Terminal Care Document." Form at 18 V.S.A. §5253. (Health care power of attorney is discussed at 14 V.S.A. §§3451 and 3452.)

FORM(S): TERMINAL CARE DOCUMENT (Form 38). Optional: Forms 45 and 46.

TYPES OF CONDITIONS: Applies to "terminal state."

DOCTOR CERTIFICATION: Not required.

FOOD & WATER: No provision.

WITNESSES: 2 witnesses; no notary.

VIRGINIA

THE LAW: Living will is part of health care power of attorney (called an "Advance Medical Directive"), Code of Virginia 1950, Title 54.1, Section 54.1-2981 (C.V. §54.1-2981). Ignore "Chapter" numbers, and look for "Title" and "Section" numbers. Form at C.V. §54.1-2984. DNR: C.V. §54.1-2987.1.

FORM(S): ADVANCE MEDICAL DIRECTIVE (Form 3). Has option to appoint health care agent. Optional: Forms 45 and 46.

TYPES OF CONDITIONS: Applies to terminal conditions.

DOCTOR CERTIFICATION: (1) Attending physician must determine the condition is terminal. (2) If a health care agent has been appointed, there must be written verification that the person is unable to make informed decisions by the attending physician and either another physician or a licensed clinical psychologist.

FOOD & WATER: No provision.

WITNESSES: 2 witnesses; no notary.

WASHINGTON

THE LAW: "Natural Death Act," *West's* Revised Code of Washington Annotated, Title 70, Chapter 122, Section 70.122.010 (R.C.W.A. §70.122.010). Form is called a "Health Care Directive." (Health care power of attorney is authorized by R.C.W.A. §§11.94.010 and 11.94.046, but no form is provided.)

FORM(S): HEALTH CARE DIRECTIVE (Form 40). Optional: Forms 45 and 46.

TYPES OF CONDITIONS: Applies to terminal or permanent unconscious conditions (these are further defined in the form).

DOCTOR CERTIFICATION: 2 physicians.

FOOD & WATER: Optional provision.

WITNESSES: 2 witnesses; no notary.

MISC.: Has pregnancy exception.

WEST VIRGINIA

THE LAW: "West Virginia Natural Death Act," West Virginia Code, Chapter 16, Article 30, Section 16-30-1 (W.V.C. §16-30-1). Living will form at W.V.C. §16-30-3. Look for 1993 Cumulative Supplement to volume 5. (Health care power of attorney provided for in the "Medical Power of Attorney Act," W.V.C. §16-30A-1. Health care power of attorney form at W.V.C. §16-30A-18. Also see the "Health Care Surrogate Act," W.V.C. §16-30B-1.) DNR: "Do Not Resuscitate Act," W.V.C. §16-30C-1 to 16; form at W.V.C. §16-30C-6.

FORM(S): LIVING WILL (Form 41). Optional: Forms 46.

TYPES OF CONDITIONS: Applies to terminal condition or persistent vegetative state.

DOCTOR CERTIFICATION: 2 physicians, one of whom is attending physician.

FOOD & WATER: No provision. However, you can insert your own provision in the paragraph for listing any special directives or limitations.

WITNESSES: 2 witnesses AND notary of signer and witnesses.

WISCONSIN

THE LAW: *West's* Wisconsin Statutes Annotated, Section 154.01 (W.S.A. §154.01). Ignore "Chapter" numbers. (Health care power of attorney form, which also includes living will provision, at W.S.A. §155.01.)

FORM(S): DECLARATION TO PHYSICIANS (Form 42). Optional: Forms 45 and 46.

TYPES OF CONDITIONS: Applies to terminal condition and persistent vegetative state.

DOCTOR CERTIFICATION: 2 physicians.

FOOD & WATER: Optional provisions.

WITNESSES: 2 witnesses; no notary.

WYOMING

THE LAW: Wyoming Statutes Annotated, Title 35, Chapter 22, Section 35-22-101 (W.S.A. §35-22-101), titled "Living Will." Living will form at W.S.A. §35-22-102. Look for volume 8. (Health care power of attorney covered at W.S.A. §3-5-201, titled "Durable Power of Attorney for Health Care," but no form provided. Look for volume 2A.)

FORM(S): DECLARATION (Form 43). Has space to designate someone to make treatment decisions for you. Optional: Forms 45 and 46.

TYPES OF CONDITIONS: Applies to terminal conditions where "death will occur whether or not life-sustaining procedures are utilized." If you think this is confusing, you are right. Here is a prime example of a legislature trying to be so comprehensive in explaining something that it makes the law unclear. As written, this form fails to accomplish a central purpose of having a living will, which is to cover the situation where a person can be kept alive indefinitely with machines or other life-sustaining procedures.

DOCTOR CERTIFICATION: 2 physicians, one of whom is the attending physician.

FOOD & WATER: No provision.

WITNESSES: 2 witnesses; no notary. Form states who may not serve as a witness.

APPENDIX B
FORMS

This appendix includes two types of living will forms: (1) statutory living will forms approved by various states, and (2) generic forms for any state not having an approved statutory form or to supplement a state form that does not have provisions you want.

The table on page 66 will help you determine which form to use for your state. The Table of Forms on pages 67 and 68 will give you the number of the form, indicate if it is for a particular state, give the title of the form, and give the page number where that form may be found. Form numbers are found at the upper, outside edge of each form. Remember, the law and forms may change at any time.

If the official form for your state does not have a provision for signature before a notary, you may want to attach Form 45 to your state form and have the signatures of yourself and your witnesses notarized. If your state's form does not have all of the provisions you would like, you may want to complete Form 46 and attach it to the state form. You may attach both Form 45 and Form 46 to your state form if necessary.

To complete Form 46, follow the instructions for Form 1 on page 28. The only difference is that, in addition to filling in your name in the first, unnumbered paragraph, you will also need to fill in the title of the living will form used in your state, and the date you signed it. For example, if you live in Maine, the title of Maine's form is "Advance Health-Care Directive," and that title will go in the space on the second line of Form 46.

Below is a state-by-state chart indicating which form to use for each state.

State	Form
Alabama	3
Alaska	4
Arizona	5
Arkansas	6
California	1
Colorado	7
Connecticut	8
Delaware	9
District of Columbia	1
Florida	10
Georgia	1
Hawaii	11
Idaho	12
Illinois	13
Indiana	14 or 15*
Iowa	16
Kansas	1
Kentucky	17
Louisiana	18
Maine	19
Maryland	20
Massachusetts	1
Michigan	1
Minnesota	21
Mississippi	22
Missouri	23

State	Form
Montana	24
Nebraska	25
Nevada	26
New Hampshire	27
New Jersey	1
New Mexico	28
New York	1
North Carolina	29
North Dakota	1
Ohio	1
Oklahoma	30
Oregon	31
Pennsylvania	1
Rhode Island	32
South Carolina	33
South Dakota	34
Tennessee	35
Texas	36
Utah	37
Vermont	38
Virginia	39
Washington	40
West Virginia	41
Wisconsin	42
Wyoming	43

*Use Form 14 to indicate that you do **not** want life-prolonging procedures; use Form 15 to indicate that you **do** want life-prolonging procedures.

TABLE OF FORMS

LIVING WILL

I, _____, being of sound mind willfully and voluntarily make known my desires regarding my medical care and treatment under the circumstances as indicated below:

_____ 1. If I should have an incurable or irreversible condition that will cause my death within a relatively short time, and if I am unable to make decisions regarding my medical treatment, I direct my attending physician to withhold or withdraw procedures that merely prolong the dying process and are not necessary to my comfort or to alleviate pain, even if such pain medication hastens death. This authorization includes, but is not limited to, the withholding or withdrawal of the following types of medical treatment (subject to any special instructions in paragraph 5 below):

    _____ a. Artificial feeding and hydration.
    _____ b. Cardiopulmonary resuscitation (this includes, but is not limited to, the use of drugs, electric shock, and artificial breathing).
    _____ c. Kidney dialysis.
    _____ d. Surgery or other invasive procedures.
    _____ e. Antibiotics.
    _____ f. Other: _____
    _____

_____ 2. If I should be in an irreversible coma or persistent vegetative state that my physicians reasonably believe to be irreversible or incurable, I direct my attending physicians to withhold or withdraw medical procedures and treatment other than such medical procedures and treatment necessary to my comfort or to alleviate pain, even if such paid medication hastens death. This authorization includes, but is not limited to, the withholding or withdrawal of the following types of medical treatment (subject to any special instructions in paragraph 5 below):

    _____ a. Artificial feeding and hydration.
    _____ b. Cardiopulmonary resuscitation (this includes, but is not limited to, the use of drugs, electric shock, and artificial breathing).
    _____ c. Kidney dialysis.
    _____ d. Surgery or other invasive procedures.
    _____ e. Antibiotics.
    _____ f. Other: _____
    _____

_____ 3. If I have a medical condition where I am unable to communicate my desires as to treatment and my physician determines that the burdens of treatment outweigh the expected benefits, I direct my attending physicians to withhold or withdraw medical procedures and treatment other than such medical procedures and treatment necessary to my comfort or to alleviate pain, even if such paid medication hastens death This authorization includes, but is not limited to, the withholding or withdrawal of the following types of medical treatment (subject to any special instructions in paragraph 5 below):

    _____ a. Artificial feeding and hydration.
    _____ b. Cardiopulmonary resuscitation (this includes, but is not limited to, the use of drugs, electric shock, and artificial breathing).
    _____ c. Kidney dialysis.

_____ d. Surgery or other invasive procedures.
_____ e. Antibiotics.
_____ f. Other: _____
            _____

_____ 4. I want my life prolonged to the greatest extent possible (subject to any special instructions in paragraph 4 below).

_____ 5. Special instructions (if any) _____
             _____
             _____
             _____

Signed this _____ day of _____,19_____.

                                        _____
                                        Signature

                                        Address:_____

                                        _____

The declarant is personally known to me and voluntarily signed this document in my presence.

Witness:_____   Witness_____

Name:_____   Name:_____

Address:_____   Address:_____

_____   _____

State of _____)
County of _____)

    On this _____ day of _____, 19_____, before me, personally appeared
_____, principal, and
_____ and _____,
witnesses, who are personally known to me or who provided _____
_____

as identification, and signed the foregoing instrument in my presence.

_____
Notary Public

REVOCATION OF LIVING WILL

I, _____

_____(name and address of principal), hereby revoke

the _____, which was executed

by me on _____. This revocation is effective immediately.

Date:_____

_____
Signature

State of _____)

County of _____)

On this _____ day of _____, 19____, before me, personally

appeared _____, who is personally known

to me or who provided _____

as identification, and signed the foregoing instrument in my presence.

_____
Notary Public

My Commission expires:

DECLARATION

Declaration made this _____ day of _____(month, year).
I, _____, being of sound mind, willfully and voluntarily make known my desire(s) that my dying shall not be artificially prolonged under the circumstances set forth below, do hereby declare:

If at any time I should have a(n) terminal condition, incurable injury, disease, or illness certified to be a terminal condition by two physicians who have personally examined me, one of whom shall be my attending physician, and the physicians have determined that my death will occur whether or not life-sustaining procedures are utilized and where the application of life-sustaining procedures would serve only to artificially prolong the dying process, I direct that such procedures be withheld or withdrawn, and that I be permitted to die naturally with only the administration of medication or the performance of any medical procedure deemed necessary to provide me with comfort care.

In the absence of my ability to give directions regarding the use of such life-sustaining procedures, it is my intention that this declaration shall be honored by my family and physician(s) as the final expression of my legal right to refuse medical or surgical treatment and accept the consequences from such refusal.

I understand the full import of this declaration and I am emotionally and mentally competent to make this declaration.

Signed_____
City, County and State of Residence_____
Date_____

The declarant has been personally known to me and I believe him or her to be of sound mind. I did not sign the declarant's signature above or at the direction of the declarant. I am not related to the declarant by blood or marriage, entitled to any portion of the estate of the declarant according to the laws of intestate succession or under any will of declarant or codicil thereto, or directly financially responsible for declarant's medical care.

Witness_____
Witness_____
Date_____

DECLARATION

If I should have an incurable or irreversible condition that will cause my death within a relatively short time, it is my desire that my life not be prolonged by administration of life-sustaining procedures.

If my condition is terminal and I am unable to participate in decisions regarding my medical treatment, I direct my attending physician to withhold or withdraw procedures that merely prolong the dying process and are not necessary to my comfort or to alleviate pain.

I [   ] do [   ] do not desire that nutrition or hydration (food and water) be provided by gastric tube or intravenously if necessary.

Signed this _____ day of _____, 19____.

Signature_____
Place_____

The declarant is known to me and voluntarily signed or voluntarily directed another to sign this document in my presence.

Witness_____

Address_____

Witness_____

Address_____

State of _____
_____Judicial District

The foregoing instrument was acknowledged before me this (date) _____ day of _____, 19_____, by (name of person who acknowledged) _____.

_____
Signature of Person Taking
Acknowledgment

_____
Title or Rank

_____
Serial Number, if any

THIS DECLARATION MUST EITHER BE WITNESSED BY TWO PERSONS OR ACKNOWL-EDGED BY A PERSON QUALIFIED TO TAKE ACKNOWLEDGMENTS UNDER A.S. §09.63.010.

HEALTH CARE POWER OF ATTORNEY

Part 1. Health Care

I, _____, as principal, designate _____ as my agent for all matters relating to my health care, including, without limitation, full power to give or refuse consent to all medical, surgical, hospital and related health care. This power of attorney is effective on my inability to make or communicate health care decisions. All of my agent's actions under this power during any period when I am unable to make or communicate health care decisions or when there is uncertainty whether I am dead or alive have the same effect on my heirs, devisees and personal representatives as if I were alive, competent and acting for myself.

If my agent is unwilling or unable to serve or continue to serve, I hereby appoint _____ as my agent.

I have _____ I have not _____ completed and attached a living will for purposes of providing specific direction to my agent in situations that may occur during any period when I am unable to make or communicate health care decisions or after my death. My agent is directed to implement those choices I have initialed in the living will.

I have _____ I have not _____ completed a prehospital medical directive pursuant to § 36-3251, Arizona Revised Statutes.

This health care directive is made under § 36-3221, Arizona Revised Statutes, and continues in effect for all who may rely on it except those to whom I have given notice of its revocation.

Part 2. Autopsy (under Arizona law an autopsy may be required)

If you wish to do so, reflect your desires below:

_____ 1. I **do not** consent to an autopsy.

_____ 2. I **consent** to an autopsy.

_____ 3. My agent **may** give consent to **or refuse** an autopsy.

Part 3. Organ Donation (Optional)

(Under Arizona law, you may make a gift of all or part of your body to a bank or storage facility or a hospital, physician or medical or dental school for transplantation, therapy, medical or dental evaluation or research or for the advancement of medical or dental science. You may also authorize your agent to do so or a member of your family to make a gift unless you give them notice that you do not want a gift made. In the space below you may make a gift yourself or state that you do not want to make a gift. If you do not complete this section, your agent will have the authority to make a gift of a part of your body pursuant to law.)

If any of the statements below reflects your desire, initial on the line next to that statement. **You do not have to initial any of the statements.**

If you do not check any of the statements, your agent and your family will have the authority to make a gift of all or part of your body under Arizona Law.

_____ I do not want to make an organ or tissue donation and do not want my agent or family to do so.

_____ I have already signed a written agreement or donor card regarding organ and tissue donation with the following individual or institution:_____

_____ Pursuant to Arizona law, I hereby give, effective on my death:

[ ] Any needed organ or parts.

[ ] The Following part or organs listed:

_____

_____

_____

for (check one):

[ ] Any legally authorized purpose.

[ ] Transplant or therapeutic purposes only.

Part 4. Physician Affidavit (Optional)

(Before initialing any choices above you may wish to ask questions of you physician regarding a particular treatment alternative. If you do speak with your physician it is a good idea to ask your physician to complete this affidavit and keep a copy for his file.)

I, Dr. _____ have reviewed this guidance document and have discussed with _____(name of principal) any questions regarding the probable medical consequences of the treatment choices provided above. This discussion with the principal occurred on _____(date).

I have agreed to comply with the provisions of this directive.

_____
Signature of physician

Part 5. Living Will (Optional)

(Some general statements concerning your health care options are outlined below. If you agree with one of the statements, you should initial that statement. **Read all of these statements carefully before you initial your selection.** You can also write your own statement concerning life-sustaining treatment and other matters relating to your health care. You may initial any combination of paragraphs 1, 2, 3 and 4, but if you initial paragraph 5 the others should not be initialed.)

_____ 1. If I have a terminal condition I **do not** want my life to be prolonged and I **do not** want life-sustaining treatment, beyond comfort care, that would serve **only** to artificially delay the moment of my death.

_____ 2. If I am in a terminal condition or an irreversible coma or a persistent vegetative state that my doctors reasonably feel to be irreversible or incurable, I **do** want the medical treatment necessary to provide care that would keep me comfortable, but I **do not** want the following:

_____ (a) Cardiopulmonary resuscitation, for example, the use of drugs, electric shock and artificial breathing.

_____ (b) Artificially administered food and fluids.

_____ (c) To be taken to a hospital if at all avoidable.

_____ 3. Notwithstanding my other directions, if I am known to be pregnant, I do not want life-sustaining treatment withheld or withdrawn if it is possible that the embryo/fetus will develop to the point of live birth with the continued application of life-sustaining treatment.

_____ 4. Notwithstanding my other directions I **do** want the use of all medical care necessary to treat my condition until my doctors reasonably conclude that my condition is terminal or is irreversible and incurable or I am in a persistent vegetative state.

_____ 5. I **want** my life to be prolonged to the greatest extent possible.

Other or additional statement of desires

I have _____ I have not _____ attached additional special provisions or limitations to this document to be honored in the absence of my being able to give health care directions.

_____
Signature of Principal

Witness:_____

Date:_____

Time:_____

_____

Address:_____

_____

_____

Address of Agent

Witness:_____

_____

Address:_____

_____

Telephone of Agent

(Note: This document may be notarized instead of being witnessed.)

State of Arizona)

County of _____)

On this _____ day of _____, 19_____ before me, personally appeared _____ (name of principal), who is personally known to me or provided _____ as identification, and acknowledged that he or she executed it.

[NOTARY SEAL]

_____
(signature of notary public)

DECLARATION

If I should have an incurable or irreversible condition that will cause my death within a relatively short time, and I am no longer able to make decisions regarding my medical treatment, I direct my attending physician, pursuant to Arkansas Rights of the Terminally Ill or Permanently Unconscious Act, to [withhold or withdraw treatment that only prolongs the process of dying and is not necessary to my comfort or to alleviate pain] [follow the instructions of _____ whom I appoint as my Health Care Proxy to decide whether life-sustaining treatment should be withheld or withdrawn].

If I should become permanently unconscious I direct my attending physician, pursuant to Arkansas Rights of the Terminally Ill or Permanently Unconscious Act, to [withhold or withdraw treatment that only prolongs the process of dying and is not necessary to my comfort or to alleviate pain] [follow the instructions of _____ _____whom I appoint as my Health Care Proxy to decide whether life-sustaining treatment should be withheld or withdrawn].

Signed this _____ day of _____, 19____.

Signature_____

Address_____

_____

The declarant voluntarily signed this writing in my presence.

Witness_____

Address_____

_____

Witness_____

Address_____

_____

DECLARATION AS TO MEDICAL OR SURGICAL TREATMENT

I, _____, being of sound mind and at least eighteen years of age, direct that my life shall not be artificially prolonged under the circumstances set forth below and hereby declare that:

    1. If at any time my attending physician and one other qualified physician certify in writing that:

    a. I have an injury, disease, or illness which is not curable or reversible and which, in their judgment, is a terminal condition, and

    b. For a period of seven consecutive days or more, I have been unconscious, comatose, or otherwise incompetent so as to be unable to make or communicate responsible decisions concerning my person, then

I direct that, in accordance with Colorado law, life-sustaining procedures shall be withdrawn and withheld pursuant to the terms of this declaration, it being understood that life-sustaining procedures shall not include any medical procedure or intervention for nourishment considered necessary by the attending physician to provide comfort or alleviate pain. However, I may specifically direct, in accordance with Colorado law, that artificial nourishment be withdrawn or withheld pursuant to the terms of this declaration.

    2. In the event that the only procedure I am being provided is artificial nourishment, I direct that one of the following actions be taken:

_____ a. Artificial nourishment shall not be continued when it is the only procedure being provided; or

_____ b. Artificial nourishment shall be continued for _____ days when it is the only procedure being provided; or

_____ c. Artificial nourishment shall be continued when it is the only procedure being provided.

    3. I execute this declaration, as my free and voluntary act, this _____ day of _____, 19___.

By_____
                                 Declarant

The foregoing instrument was signed and declared by _____ to be his declaration, in the presence of us, who, in his presence, in the presence of each other, and at his request, have signed our names below as witnesses, and we declare that, at the time of the execution of this instrument, the declarant, according to our best knowledge and belief, was of sound mind and under no constraint or undue influence.

Dated at _____, Colorado, this _____ day of _____, 19___.

_____
Name and Address of Witness

_____
Name and Address of Witness

STATE OF COLORADO   )
) ss.
COUNTY OF _____)

    SUBSCRIBED and sworn to before me by _____, the declarant, and _____ and _____, witnesses, as the voluntary act and deed of the declarant the _____ day of _____, 19____.
My commission expires:

_____
                                Notary Public

DOCUMENT CONCERNING WITHHOLDING OR WITHDRAWAL
OF LIFE SUPPORT SYSTEMS

If the time comes when I am incapacitated to the point when I can no longer actively take part in decisions for my own life, and am unable to direct my physicians as to my own medical care, I wish this statement to stand as a testament of my wishes.

I, _____ (Name), request that, if my condition is deemed terminal or if it is determined that I will be permanently unconscious, I be allowed to die and not be kept alive through life support systems. By terminal condition, I mean that I have an incurable or irreversible medical condition which, without the administration of life support systems, will, in the opinion of my attending physician, result in death within a relatively short time. By permanently unconscious I mean that I am in a permanent coma or persistent vegetative state which is an irreversible condition in which I am at no time aware of myself or the environment and show no behavioral response to the environment. The life support systems which I do not want include, but are not limited to:

- Artificial respiration
- Cardiopulmonary resuscitation
- Artificial means of providing nutrition and hydration

(Cross out and initial life support systems you want administered)

I do not intend any direct taking of my life, but only that my dying not be unreasonably prolonged.

Other specific requests: _____

_____.

This request is made, after careful reflection, while I am of sound mind.

_____ Signature

_____ Date

This document was signed in our presence, by the above-named _____ (Name) who appeared to be eighteen years of age or older, of sound mind and able to understand the nature and consequences of health care decisions at the time the document was signed.

_____ Witness   _____ Witness

_____ Address   _____ Address

ADVANCE HEALTH-CARE DIRECTIVE

EXPLANATION

You have the right to give instructions about your own health care. You also have the right to name someone else to make health-care decisions for you. This form lets you do either or both of these things. It also lets you express your wishes regarding anatomical gifts and the designation of your primary physician. If you use this form, you may complete or modify all or any part of it. You are free to use a different form.

Part 1 of this form is a power of attorney for health care. Part 1 lets you name another individual as agent to make health-care decisions for you if you become incapable of making your own decisions. You may also name an alternate agent to act for you if your first choice is not willing, able or reasonably available to make decisions for you. Unless related to you, an agent may not have a controlling interest in or be an operator or employee of a residential long-term health-care institution at which you are receiving care. If you do not have a qualifying condition (terminal illness/injury or permanent unconsciousness), your agent may make all health-care decisions for you except for decisions providing, withholding or withdrawing of a life sustaining procedure. Unless you limit the agent's authority, your agent will have the right to:

(a) Consent or refuse consent to any care, treatment, service or procedure to maintain, diagnose or otherwise affect a physical or mental condition unless it's a life-sustaining procedure or otherwise required by law.

(b) Select or discharge health-care providers and health-care institutions;

If you have a qualifying condition, your agent may make all health-care decisions for you, including, but not limited to:

(c) The decisions listed in (a) and (b).

(d) Consent or refuse consent to life sustaining procedures, such as, but not limited to, cardiopulmonary resuscitation and orders not to resuscitate.

(e) Direct the providing, withholding or withdrawal of artificial nutrition and hydration and all other forms of health care.

Part 2 of this form lets you give specific instructions about any aspect of your health care. Choices are provided for you to express your wishes regarding the provision, withholding or withdrawal of treatment to keep you alive, including the provision of artificial nutrition and hydration as well as the provision of pain relief. Space is also provided for you to add to the choices you have made or for you to write out any additional instructions for other than end of life decisions.

Part 3 of this form lets you express an intention to donate your bodily organs and tissues following your death.

Part 4 of this form lets you designate a physician to have primary responsibility for your health care.

After completing this form, sign and date the form at the end. It is required that 2 other individuals sign as witnesses. Give a copy of the signed and completed form to your physician, to any other health-care providers you may have, to any health-care institution at which you are receiving care and to any health-care agents you have named. You should talk to the person you have named as agent to make sure that the person understands your wishes and is willing to take the responsibility.

You have the right to revoke this advance health-care directive or replace this form at any time.

* * * * * * * * * * * * * * * * * * * *

PART 1: POWER OF ATTORNEY FOR HEALTH CARE

(1) DESIGNATION OF AGENT: I designate the following individual as my agent to make health-care decisions for me:

_____

(name of individual you choose as agent)

(address)	(city)	(state)	(zip code)

(home phone)	(work phone)

OPTIONAL: If I revoke my agent's authority or if my agent is not willing, able or reasonably available to make a health-care decision for me, I designate as my first alternate agent:

_____
(name of individual you choose as first alternate agent)

(address)	(city)	(state)	(zip code)

(home phone)	(work phone)

OPTIONAL: If I revoke the authority of my agent and first alternate agent or if neither is willing, able or reasonably available to make a health-care decision for me, I designate as my second alternate agent:

_____
(name of individual you choose as second alternate agent)

(address)	(city)	(state)	(zip code)

(home phone)	(work phone)

(2) AGENT'S AUTHORITY: If I am not in a qualifying condition my agent is authorized to make all health-care decisions for me, except decisions about life-sustaining procedures and as I state here; and if I am in a qualifying condition, my agent is authorized to make all health-care decisions for me, except as I state here:

_____
_____
_____
(Add additional sheets if needed.)

(3) WHEN AGENT'S AUTHORITY BECOMES EFFECTIVE: My agent's authority becomes effective when my primary physician determines I lack the capacity to make my own health-care decisions. As to decisions concerning the providing, withholding and withdrawal of life-sustaining procedures my agent's authority becomes effective when my primary physician determines I lack the capacity to make my own health-care decisions and my primary physician and another physician determine that I am in a terminal condition or permanently unconscious.

(4) AGENT'S OBLIGATIONS: My agent shall make health-care decisions for me in accordance with this power of attorney for health care, any instructions I give in Part 2 of this form, and my other wishes to the extent known to my agent. To the extent my wishes are unknown, my agent shall make health-care decisions for me in accordance with what my agent determines to be in my best interest. In determining my best interest, my agent shall consider my personal values to the extent known to my agent.

(5) NOMINATION OF GUARDIAN: If a guardian of my person needs to be appointed for me by a court, (please check one):
[   ]   I nominate the agent(s) whom I named in this form in the order designated to act as guardian.

[   ]   I nominate the following to be guardian in the order designated:

_____

_____

[   ]   I do not nominate anyone to be guardian.

PART 2. INSTRUCTIONS FOR HEALTH CARE

If you are satisfied to allow your agent to determine what is best for you in making end-of-life decisions, you need not fill out this part of the form. If you do fill out this part of the form, you may strike any wording you do not want.

(6) END-OF-LIFE DECISIONS: If I am in a qualifying condition, I direct that my health-care providers and others involved in my care provide, withhold, or withdraw treatment in accordance with the choice I have marked below:

Choice Not To Prolong Life

I do not want my life to be prolonged if: (please check all that apply)

_____ (i)   I have a terminal condition (an incurable condition caused by injury, disease, or illness which, to a reasonable degree of medical certainty, makes death imminent and from which, despite the application of life-sustaining procedures, there can be no recovery) and regarding artificial nutrition and hydration,

I make the following specific directions:	I want used	I do not want used
Artificial nutrition through a conduit	_____	_____
Hydration through a conduit	_____	_____

_____(ii)   I become permanently unconscious (a medical condition that has been diagnosed in accordance with currently accepted medical standards that has lasted at least 4 weeks and with reasonable medical certainty as total and irreversible loss of consciousness and capacity for interaction with the environment. The term includes, without limitation, a persistent vegetative state or irreversible coma) and regarding artificial nutrition and hydration,

I make the following specific directions:	I want used	I do not want used
Artificial nutrition through a conduit	_____	_____
Hydration through a conduit	_____	_____

Choice To Prolong Life

_____   I want my life to be prolonged as long as possible within the limits of generally accepted health-care standards.

RELIEF FROM PAIN: Except as I state in the following space, I direct treatment for alleviation of pain or discomfort be provided at all times, even if it hastens my death: _____

_____

_____

(7) OTHER MEDICAL INSTRUCTIONS: (If you do not agree with any of the optional choices above and wish to write you own, or if you wish to add to the instructions you have given above, you may do so here.) I direct that:

_____

_____

(Add additional sheets if necessary.)

PART 3: ANATOMICAL GIFTS AT DEATH

(OPTIONAL)

(8) I am mentally competent and 18 years or more of age.

I hereby make this anatomical gift to take effect upon my death. The marks in the appropriate squares and words filled into the blanks below indicate my desires.

I give: [   ] my body;   [   ] any needed organs or parts;

[   ] the following organs or parts: _____

To the following person or institutions:

[   ] the physician in attendance at my death;

[   ] the hospital in which I die;

[   ] the following named physician, hospital, storage bank or other medical institution:

_____

[   ] the following individual for treatment:

_____

for the following purposes: [   ] any purpose authorized by law;   [   ] transplantation;

[   ] therapy;   [   ] research;   [   ] medical education.

PART 4: PRIMARY PHYSICIAN

(9) I designate the following physician as my primary physician:

_____

(name of physician)   (phone)

_____

(address)   (city)   (state)   (zip code)

OPTIONAL: If the physician I have designated above is not willing, able or reasonably available to act as my primary physician, I designate the following physician as my primary physician:

_____

(name of physician)   (phone)

_____

(address)   (city)   (state)   (zip code)

Primary Physician shall mean a physician designated by an individual or the individual's agent or guardian, to have primary responsibility for the individual's health care or, in the absence of a designation or if the designated physician is not reasonably available, a physician who undertakes the responsibility.

* * * * * * * * * * * * * * * * * * *

(10)   EFFECT OF COPY: A copy of this form has the same effect as the original.

(11)   SIGNATURE: Sign and date the form here: I understand the purposes and effect of this document.

_____   _____

(date)   (sign your name)

_____   _____

(address)   (print your name)

_____

(city)   (state)   (zip code)

(12) SIGNATURE OF WITNESSES:

Statement Of Witnesses

SIGNED AND DECLARED by the above-named declarant as and for his/her written declaration under 16 Del.C. §§ 2502 and 2503, in our presence, who in his/her presence, at his/her request, and in the presence of each other, have hereunto subscribed our names as witnesses, and state:

A. That the Declarant is mentally competent.

B. That neither of them:

1. Is related to the declarant by blood, marriage or adoption;

2. Is entitled to any portion of the estate of the declarant under any will of the declarant or codicil thereto then existing nor, at the time of the executing of the advance health care directive, is so entitled by operation of law then existing;

3. Has, at the time of the execution of the advance health-care directive, a present or inchoate claim against any portion of the estate of the declarant;

4. Has a direct financial responsibility for the declarant's medical care;

5. Has a controlling interest in or is an operator or an employee of a residential long-term health-care institution in which the declarant is a resident; or

6. Is under eighteen years of age.

C. That if the declarant is a resident of a sanitarium, rest home, nursing home, boarding home or related institution, one of the witnesses, _____, is at the time of the execution of the advance health-care directive, a patient advocate or ombudsman designated by the Division of Services for Aging and Adults with Physical Disabilities or the Public Guardian.

First witness	Second witness
_____	_____
(print name)	(print name)
_____	_____
(address)	(address)
_____	_____
(city) (state)	(city) (state)
_____	_____
(signature of witness)	(signature of witness)
_____	_____
(date)	(date)

LIVING WILL

Declaration made this _____ day of _____, 19____.

I, _____, willfully and voluntarily make known my desire that my dying not be artificially prolonged under the circumstances set forth below, and I do hereby declare:

If at any time I have a terminal condition and if my attending or treating physician and another consulting physician have determined that there is no medical probability of my recovery from such condition, I direst that life-prolonging procedures be withheld or withdrawn when the application of such procedures would serve only to prolong artificially the process of dying, and that I be permitted to die naturally with only the administration of medication or the performance of any medical procedure deemed necessary to provide me with comfort care or to alleviate pain.

It is my intention that this declaration be honored by my family and physician as the final expression of my legal right to refuse medical or surgical treatment and to accept the consequences for such refusal.

In the event that I have been determined to be unable to provide express and informed consent regarding the withholding, withdrawal, or continuation of life-prolonging procedures, I wish to designate, as my surrogate to carry out the provisions of this declaration:

Name: _____

Address: _____

_____Zip Code: _____

Phone: _____

I understand the full import of this declaration, and I am emotionally and mentally competent to make this declaration.

Additional Instructions (optional): _____

_____

_____

Signature

Witness: _____   Witness: _____

Name: _____   Name: _____

Address: _____   Address: _____

_____   _____

Phone: _____   Phone: _____

DECLARATION

A.   Statement of Declarant

Declaration made this _____ day of _____ (month, year). I,
_____, being of sound mind, and understanding
that I have the right to request that my life be prolonged to the greatest extent possible, wilfully and voluntarily make known my desire that my dying shall not be artificially prolonged under the circumstances set forth
below, and do hereby declare:

My instructions shall prevail even if they create a conflict with the desires of my relatives, hospital policies, or the principles of those providing my care.

If I should develop a terminal condition or a permanent loss of the ability to communicate concerning
medical treatment decisions, with no reasonable chance of regaining this ability, I do not want to have my life
prolonged. I would not want to be subjected to surgery or resuscitation. Nor would I then wish to have life sustaining medicine or procedures. Instead, I request care, including medicine and procedures, for the purpose of
providing comfort and pain relief.

CHECKLIST

I have also considered whether I want tube feeding to be provided and have selected one of the following provisions by putting a mark in the space provided:

(   ) I do NOT want my life prolonged by tube or other artificial feeding or provision of fluids by a
         tube if my condition is as stated above.

(   ) I DO want my life prolonged by tube or other artificial feeding and provision of fluids by a tube
         if my condition is as stated above.

If neither provision is selected or if both are selected, it shall be presumed that tube or other artificial feeding
or provision of fluids by tube are requested to prolong the declarant's life.

This declaration shall control in all circumstances.

I understand the full import of this declaration and I am emotionally and mentally competent to make
this declaration.

Signed_____
Address_____
_____

B.	Statement of Witness

I am at least 18 years of age and
-not related to the principal by blood, marriage, or adoption; and
-not currently the attending physician, an employee of the attending physician, or an employee of the health care facility in which the principal is a patient.

The declarant is personally known to me and I believe the declarant to be of sound mind.

Witness_____

Address_____

_____

Witness_____

Address_____

_____

C.	Notarization

Subscribed, sworn to and acknowledged before me by _____, the declarant, and subscribed and sworn to before me by _____ and _____, witnesses, this _____ day of _____, 19____.

Signed_____

_____

(Official capacity of officer)

A LIVING WILL

A Directive to Withhold or to Provide Treatment

To my family, my relatives, my friends, my physicians, my employers, and all others whom it may concern:

Directive made this _____ day of _____, 19_____, I, _____ _____(name), being of sound mind, willfully, and voluntarily make known my desire that my life shall not be prolonged artificially under the circumstances set forth below, do hereby declare:

1.   If at any time I should have an incurable injury, disease, illness or condition certified to be terminal by two medical doctors who have examined me, and where the application of life-sustaining procedures of any kind would serve only to prolong artificially the moment of my death, and where a medical doctor determines that my death is imminent, whether or not life-sustaining procedures are utilized, or I have been diagnosed as being in a persistent vegetative state, I direct that the following marked expressions of my intent be followed and that I be permitted to die naturally, and that I receive any medical treatment or care that may be required to keep me free of pain or distress.

Check One Box

o   If at any time I should become unable to communicate my instructions, then I direct that all medical treatment, care, and nutrition and hydration necessary to restore my health, sustain my life, and to abolish or alleviated pain or distress be provided to me. Nutrition and hydration shall not be withheld or withdrawn from me if I would die from malnutrition or dehydration rather than from my injury, disease, illness or condition.

o   If at any time I should become unable to communicate my instructions and where the application of artificial life-sustaining procedures shall serve only to prolong artificially the moment of my death, I direct such procedures be withheld or withdrawn except for the administration of nutrition and hydration.

o   If at any time I should become unable to communicate my instructions and where the application of artificial life-sustaining procedures shall serve only to prolong artificially the moment of death, I direct such procedures be withheld or withdrawn including withdrawal of the administration of nutrition and hydration.

2.   In the absence of my ability to give directions regarding the use of life-sustaining procedures, I hereby appoint _____ (name) currently residing at _____, as my attorney-in-fact/proxy for the making of decisions relating to my health care in my place; and it is my intention that this appointment shall be honored by him/her, by my family, relatives, friends, physicians and lawyer as the final expression of my legal right to refuse medical or surgical treatment; and I accept the consequences of such a decision. I have duly executed a Durable Power of Attorney for health care decisions on this date.

3.   In the absence of my ability to give further directions regarding my treatment, including life-sustaining procedures, it is my intention that this directive shall be honored by my family and physicians as the final expression of my legal right to refuse or accept medical and surgical treatment, and I accept the consequences of such refusal.

4.   If I have been diagnosed as pregnant and that diagnosis is known to any interested person, this directive shall have no force during the course of my pregnancy.

5.   I understand the full importance of this directive and am emotionally and mentally competent to make this directive. No participant in the making of this directive or in its being carried into effect, whether it be a medical doctor, my spouse, a relative, friend or any other person shall be held responsible in any way, legally, professionally or socially, for complying with my directions.

Signed _____

City, county and state of residence _____

The declarant has been known to me personally and I believe him/her to be of sound mind.

Witness _____   Witness _____

Address _____   Address _____

_____   _____

DECLARATION

This declaration is made this _____ day of _____ (month, year). I, _____, being of sound mind, willfully and voluntarily make known my desires that my moment of death shall not be artificially postponed.

If at any time I should have an incurable and irreversible injury, disease, or illness judged to be a terminal condition by my attending physician who has personally examined me and has determined that my death is imminent except for death delaying procedures, I direct that such procedures which would only prolong the dying process be withheld or withdrawn, and that I be permitted to die naturally with only the administration of medication, sustenance, or the performance of any medical procedure deemed necessary by my attending physician to provide me with comfort care.

In the absence of my ability to give directions regarding the use of such death delaying procedures, it is my intention that this declaration shall be honored by my family and physician as the final expression of my legal right to refuse medical or surgical treatment and accept the consequences from such refusal.

Signed _____

City, County and State of Residence _____

The declarant is personally known to me and I believe him or her to be of sound mind. I saw the declarant sign the declaration in my presence (or the declarant acknowledged in my presence that he or she had signed the declaration) and I signed the declaration as a witness in the presence of the declarant. I did not sign the declarant's signature above for or at the direction of the declarant. At the date of this instrument, I am not entitled to any portion of the estate of the declarant according to the laws of intestate succession or, to the best of my knowledge and belief, under any will or declarant or other instrument taking effect at declarant's death, or directly financially responsible for declarant's medical care.

Witness _____

Witness _____

LIVING WILL DECLARATION

Declaration made this _____ day of _____ (month, year). I, _____, being at least eighteen (18) years of age and of sound mind, willfully, and voluntarily make known my desires that my dying shall not be artificially prolonged under the circumstances set forth below, and I declare:

If at any time I have an incurable injury, disease, or illness certified in writing to be a terminal condition by my attending physician, and my attending physician has determined that my death will occur within a short time, and the use of life prolonging procedures would serve only to artificially prolong the dying process, I direct that such procedures be withheld or withdrawn and that I be permitted to die naturally with only the provision of appropriate nutrition and hydration and the administration of medication and the performance of any medical procedure necessary to provide me with comfort care or to alleviate pain.

In the absence of my ability to give directions regarding the use of life prolonging procedures, it is my intention that this declaration be honored by my family and physician as the final expression of my legal right to refuse medical or surgical treatment and accept the consequences of the refusal.

I understand the full import of this declaration.

Signed_____

_____
City, County, and State of Residence

The declarant has been personally known to me, and I believe (him/her) to be of sound mind. I did not sign the declarant's signature above for or at the direction of the declarant. I am not a parent, spouse, or child of the declarant. I am not entitled to any part of the declarant's estate or directly financially responsible for the declarant's medical care. I am competent and at least eighteen (18) years of age.

Witness_____   Date_____

Witness _____   Date_____

LIFE PROLONGING PROCEDURES DECLARATION

Declaration made this _____ day of _____(month, year).
I,_____, being at least eighteen (18) years of age and of sound mind, willfully and voluntarily make known my desire that if at any time I have an incurable injury, disease, or illness determined to be a terminal condition I request the use of life prolonging procedures that would extend my life. This includes appropriate nutrition and hydration, the administration of medication, and the performance of all other medical procedures necessary to extend my life, to provide comfort care, or to alleviate pain.

In the absence of my ability to give directions regarding the use of life prolonging procedures, it is my intention that this declaration be honored by my family and physician as the final expression of my legal right to request medical or surgical treatment and accept the consequences of the request.

I understand the full import of this declaration.

Signed _____

_____
City, County, and State of Residence

The declarant has been personally known to me, and I believe (him/her) to be of sound mind. I am competent and at least eighteen (18) years of age.

Witness_____ Date_____

Witness _____ Date_____

Living Will

If I should have an incurable or irreversible condition that will result either in death within a relatively short period of time or a state of permanent unconsciousness from which, to a reasonable degree of medical certainty, there can be no recovery, it is my desire that my life not be prolonged by the administration of life-sustaining procedures. If I am unable to participate in my health care decisions, I direct my attending physician to withhold or withdraw life-sustaining procedures that merely prolong the dying process and are not necessary to my comfort or freedom from pain.

Date _____ _____
Signature

Witness: _____

Witness: _____

Living Will Directive

My wishes regarding life-prolonging treatment and artificially provided nutrition and hydration to be provided to me if I no longer have decisional capacity, have a terminal condition, or become permanently unconscious have been indicated by checking and initialing the appropriate lines below. By checking and initialing the appropriate lines, I specifically:

_____ Designate _____ as my health care surrogate(s) to make health care decisions for me in accordance with this directive when I no longer have decisional capacity. If _____ refuses or is not able to act for me, I designate _____ as my health care surrogate(s).

Any prior designation is revoked.

If I do not designate a surrogate, the following are my directions to my attending physician. If I have designated a surrogate, my surrogate shall comply with my wishes as indicated below:

_____ Direct that treatment be withheld or withdrawn, and that I be permitted to die naturally with only the administration of medication or the performance of any medical treatment deemed necessary to alleviate pain.

_____ DO NOT authorize that life-prolonging treatment be withheld or withdrawn.

_____ Authorize the withholding or withdrawal of artificially provided food, water, or other artificially provided nourishment or fluids.

_____ DO NOT authorize the withholding or withdrawal of artificially provided food, water, or other artificially provided nourishment or fluids.

_____ Authorize my surrogate, designated above, to withhold or withdraw artificially provided nourishment or fluids, or other treatment if the surrogate determines that withholding or withdrawing is in my best interest; but I do not mandate that withholding or withdrawing.

In the absence of my ability to give direction regarding the use of life-prolonging treatment and artificially provided nutrition and hydration, it is my intention that this directive shall be honored by my attending physician, my family, and any surrogate designated pursuant to this directive as the final expression of my legal right to refuse medical or surgical treatment and I accept the consequences of the refusal.

If I have been diagnosed as pregnant and that diagnosis is known to my attending physician, this directive shall have no force or effect during the course of my pregnancy.

I understand the full import of this directive and I am emotionally and mentally competent to make this directive.

Signed this _____ day of _____, 19_____.

_____

Signature

_____

Address

In our joint presence, the grantor, who is of sound mind and eighteen (18) years of age, or older, voluntarily dated and signed this writing or directed it to be dated and signed for the grantor.

_____   _____

Signature of witness   Signature of witness

_____   _____

Address   Address

OR

STATE OF KENTUCKY   )

_____ COUNTY   )

Before me, the undersigned authority, came the grantor who is of sound mind and eighteen (18) years of age, or older, and acknowledged that he voluntarily dated and signed this writing or directed it to be signed and dated as above.

Done this _____ day of _____, 19_____.

_____

Signature of Notary Public or other officer

Date commission expires: _____

Execution of this document restricts withholding and withdrawing of some medical procedures. Consult Kentucky Revised Statutes or your attorney.

DECLARATION

Declaration made this _____ day of _____ (month, year).

I, _____, being of sound mind, willfully and voluntarily make known my desire that my dying shall not be artificially prolonged under the circumstances set forth below and do hereby declare:

If at any time I should have an incurable injury, disease or illness, or be in a continual profound comatose state with no reasonable chance of recovery, certified to be a terminal and irreversible condition by two physicians who have personally examined me, one of whom shall be my attending physician, and the physicians have determined that my death will occur whether or not life-sustaining procedures are utilized and where the application of life-sustaining procedure would serve only to prolong artificially the dying process, I direct that such procedures be withheld or withdrawn and that I be permitted to die naturally with only the administration of medication or the performance of any medical procedure deemed necessary to provide me with comfort care.

In the absence of my ability to give directions regarding the use of such life-sustaining procedures, it is my intention that this declaration shall be honored by my family and physician(s) as the final expression of my legal right to refuse medical or surgical treatment and accept the consequences from such refusal.

I understand the full import of this declaration and I am emotionally and mentally competent to make this declaration.

Signed_____

City, Parish and State of Residence_____

The declarant has been personally known to me and I believe him or her to be of sound mind.

Witness_____

Witness_____

ADVANCE HEALTH-CARE DIRECTIVE

Explanation

You have the right to give instructions about your own health care. You also have the right to name someone else to make health-care decisions for you. This form lets you do either or both of these things. It also lets you express your wishes regarding donation of organs and the designation of your primary physician. If you use this form, you may complete or modify all or any part of it. You are free to use a different form.

Part 1 of this form is a power of attorney for health care. Part 1 lets you name another individual as agent to make health-care decisions for you if you become incapable of making your own decisions or if you want someone else to make those decisions for you now even though you are still capable. You may also name an alternate agent to act for you if your first choice is not willing, able or reasonably available to make decisions for you. Unless related to you, your agent may not be an owner, operator or employee of a residential long-term health-care institution at which you are receiving care.

Unless the form you sign limits the authority of your agent, your agent may make all health-care decisions for you. This form has a place for you to limit the authority of your agent. You need not limit the authority of your agent if you wish to rely on your agent for all health-care decisions that may have to be made. If you choose not to limit the authority of your agent, your agent will have the right to:

(a) Consent or refuse consent to any care, treatment, service or procedure to maintain, diagnose or otherwise affect a physical or mental condition;

(b) Select or discharge health-care providers and institutions.

(c) Approve or disapprove diagnostic tests, surgical procedures, programs of medication and orders not to resuscitate; and

(d) Direct the provision, withholding or withdrawal of artificial nutrition and hydration and all other forms of health care, including life-sustaining treatment.

Part 2 of this form lets you give specific instructions about any aspect of your health care. Choices are provided for you to express your wishes regarding the provision, withholding or withdrawal of treatment to keep you alive, including the provision of artificial nutrition and hydration, as well as the provision of pain relief. Space is also provided for you to add to the choices you have made or for you to write out any additional wishes.

Part 3 of this form lets you express an intention to donate your bodily organs and tissues following your death.

Part 4 of this form lets you designate a physician to have primary responsibility for your health care.

After completing this form, sign and date the form at the end. You must have 2 other individuals sign as witnesses. Give a copy of the signed and completed form to your physician, to any other health-care providers you may have, to any health-care institution at which you are receiving care and to any health-care agents you have named. You should talk to the person you have named as agent to make sure that he or she understands your wishes and is willing to take the responsibility.

You have the right to revoke this advance health-care directive or replace this form at any time.

* * * * * * * * * * * * * * * * * * *

PART 1. POWER OF ATTORNEY FOR HEALTH CARE

(1) DESIGNATION OF AGENT: I designate the following individual as my agent to make health-care decisions for me:

_____
(name of individual you choose as agent)

_____
(address)   (city)   (state)   (zip code)

_____
(home phone)   (work phone)

OPTIONAL: If I revoke my agent's authority or if my agent is not willing, able or reasonably available to make a health-care decision for me, I designate as my first alternate agent:

_____
(name of individual you choose as first alternate agent)

_____
(address)   (city)   (state)   (zip code)

_____
(home phone)   (work phone)

OPTIONAL: If I revoke the authority of my agent and first alternate agent or if neither is willing, able or reasonably available to make a health-care decision for me, I designate as my second alternate agent:

_____
(name of individual you choose as second alternate agent)

_____
(address)   (city)   (state)   (zip code)

_____
(home phone)   (work phone)

(2) AGENT'S AUTHORITY: My agent is authorized to make all health-care decisions for me, including decisions to provide, withhold or withdraw artificial nutrition and hydration and all other forms of health care to keep me alive, except as I state here:

_____
_____
_____
(Add additional sheets if needed)

(3) WHEN AGENT'S AUTHORITY BECOMES EFFECTIVE: My agent's authority becomes effective when my primary physician determines that I am unable to make my own health-care decisions unless I mark the following box. If I mark this box [   ], my agent's authority to make health-care decisions for me takes effect immediately.

(4) AGENT'S OBLIGATION: My agent shall make health-care decisions for me in accordance with this power of attorney for health care, any instructions I give in Part 2 of this form and my other wishes to the extent known to my agent. To the extent my wishes are unknown, my agent shall make health-care decisions for me in accordance with what my agent determines to be in my best interest. In determining my best interest, my agent shall consider my personal values to the extent known to my agent.

(5) NOMINATION OF GUARDIAN: If a guardian of my person needs to be appointed for me by a court, I nominate the agent designated in this form. If that agent is not willing, able or reasonably available to act as guardian, I nominate the alternate agents whom I have named, in the order designated.

PART 2. INSTRUCTIONS FOR HEALTH CARE
If you are satisfied to allow your agent to determine what is best for you in making end-of-life decisions, you need not fill out this part of the form. If you do fill out this part of the form, you may strike any wording you do not want.

(6) END-OF-LIFE DECISIONS: I direct that my health-care providers and others involved in my care provide, withhold or withdraw treatment in accordance with the choice I have marked below:

    [ ] (a) Choice Not To Prolong Life: I do not want my life to be prolonged if (i) I have an incurable and irreversible condition that will result in my death within a relatively short time, (ii) I become unconscious and, to a reasonable degree of medical certainty, I will not regain consciousness, or (iii) the likely risks and burdens of treatment would outweigh the expected benefits, OR

    [ ] (b) Choice To Prolong Life: I want my life to be prolonged as long as possible within the limits of generally accepted health-care standards.

(7) ARTIFICIAL NUTRITION AND HYDRATION: Artificial nutrition and hydration must be provided, withheld or withdrawn in accordance with the choice I have made in paragraph (6) unless I mark the following box. If I mark this box [ ], artificial nutrition and hydration must be provided regardless of my condition and regardless of the choice I have made in paragraph (6).

(8) RELIEF FROM PAIN: Except as I state in the following space, I direct that treatment for alleviation of pain or discomfort be provided at all times, even if it hastens my death:

_____

_____

(9) OTHER WISHES: (If you do not agree with any of the optional choices above and wish to write your own, or if you wish to add to the instructions you have given above, you may do so here.) I direct that:

_____

(Add additional sheets if needed)

PART 3. DONATION OF ORGANS AT DEATH (OPTIONAL)

(10) Upon my death (mark applicable box)

    [ ] (a) I give needed organs, tissues or parts OR

    [ ] (b) I give the following organs, tissues or parts only

    _____

    [ ] (c) My gift is for the following purposes (strike any of the following you do not want)

        (i)   Transplant

        (ii)   Therapy

        (iii) Research

        (iv) Education

PART 4. PRIMARY PHYSICIAN (OPTIONAL)

(11)   I designate the following physician as my primary physician:

_____

    (name of physician)   (phone)

_____

    (address)   (city)   (state)   (zip code)

OPTIONAL: If the physician I have designated above is not willing, able or reasonably available to act as my primary physician, I designate the following physician as my primary physician:

_____

    (name of physician)   (phone)

_____

    (address)   (city)   (state)   (zip code)

* * * * * * * * * * * * * * * * * * *

(12)   EFFECT OF COPY: A copy of this form has the same effect as the original.

(13)   SIGNATURES: Sign and date the form here:

_____   _____
              (date)   (sign your name)

_____   _____
            (address)   (print your name)

_____
      (city)   (state)

(Optional) SIGNATURES OF WITNESSES:

              First witness   Second witness

_____   _____
           (print name)   (print name)

_____   _____
            (address)   (address)

_____   _____
      (city   (state)   (city)   (state)

_____   _____
       (signature of witness)   (signature of witness)

_____   _____
              (date)   (date)

HEALTH CARE DECISION MAKING FORMS

The following form allows you to make some decisions about future health care issues. The form, called a "living will," allows you to make decisions about life-sustaining procedures if, in the future, your death from a terminal condition is imminent despite the application of life-sustaining procedures or you are in a persistent vegetative state.

This form is intended to be a guide. You may complete all or only part of the form that you use. Different forms may also be used.

Please note: If you decide to select a health care agent that person may not be a witness to your advance directive. Also, at least one of your witnesses may not be a person who may financially benefit by reason of your death.

Living Will
(Optional Form)

If I am not able to make an informed decision regarding my health care, I direct my health care providers to follow my instructions as set forth below. (Initial those statements you wish to be included in the document and cross through those statements which do not apply.)

a.   If my death from a terminal condition is imminent and even if life-sustaining procedures are used there is no reasonable expectation of my recovery —

_____I direct that my life not be extended by life-sustaining procedures, including the administration of nutrition and hydration artificially.

_____I direct that my life not be extended by life-sustaining procedures, except that, if I am unable to take food by mouth, I wish to receive nutrition and hydration artificially.

_____I direct that, even in a terminal condition, I be given all available medical treatment in accordance with accepted health care standards.

b.   If I am in a persistent vegetative state, that is if I am not conscious and am not aware of my environment nor able to interact with others, and there is no reasonable expectation of my recovery within a medically appropriate period —

_____I direct that my life not be extended by life-sustaining procedures, including the administration of nutrition and hydration artificially.

_____I direct that my life not be extended by life-sustaining procedures, except that, if I am unable to take food by mouth, I wish to receive nutrition and hydration artificially.

_____I direct that I be given all available medical treatment in accordance with accepted health care standards.

c.   If I am pregnant my health care providers shall follow these specific instructions: _____
_____
_____
_____

By signing below, I indicate that I am emotionally and mentally competent to make this living will and that I understand its purpose and effect.

_____   _____
(Date)   (Signature of Declarant)

The declarant signed or acknowledged signing this living will in my presence and based upon my personal observation the declarant appears to be a competent individual.

_____   _____
(Witness)   (Witness)

(Signature of Two Witnesses)

HEALTH CARE LIVING WILL

Notice:

This is an important legal document. Before signing this document, you should know these important facts:

(a) This document gives your health care providers or your designated proxy the power and guidance to make health care decisions according to your wishes when you are in a terminal condition and cannot do so. This document may include what kind of treatment you want or do not want and under what circumstances you want these decisions to be made. You may state where you want or do not want to receive any treatment.

(b) If you name a proxy in this document and that person agrees to serve as your proxy, that person has a duty to act consistently with your wishes. If the proxy does not know your wishes, the proxy has the duty to act in your best interests. If you do not name a proxy, your health care providers have a duty to act consistently with your instructions or tell you that they are unwilling to do so.

(c) This document will remain valid and in effect until and unless you amend or revoke it. Review this document periodically to make sure it continues to reflect your preferences. You may amend or revoke the living will at any time by notifying your health care providers.

(d) Your named proxy has the same right as you have to examine your medical records and to consent to their disclosure for purposes related to your health care or insurance unless you limit this right in this document.

(e) If there is anything in this document that you do not understand, you should ask for professional help to have it explained to you.

TO MY FAMILY, DOCTORS, AND ALL THOSE CONCERNED WITH MY CARE:

I, _____ , born on _____ , 19_____ (birthdate), being an adult of sound mind, willfully and voluntarily make this statement as a directive to be followed if I am in a terminal condition and become unable to participate in decisions regarding my health care. I understand that my health care providers are legally bound to act consistently with my wishes, within the limits of reasonable medical practice and other applicable law. I also understand that I have the right to make medical and health care decisions for myself as long as I am able to do so and to revoke this living will at any time.

(1) The following are my feelings and wishes regarding my health care (you may state the circumstances under which this living will applies):

_____
_____
_____
_____

(2) I particularly want to have all appropriate health care that will help in the following ways (you may give instructions for care you do want):

_____
_____
_____
_____

(3) I particularly do not want the following (you may list specific treatment you do not want in certain circumstances):

_____
_____

(4) I particularly want to have the following kinds of life-sustaining treatment if I am diagnosed to

have a terminal condition (you may list the specific types of life-sustaining treatment that you do want if you have a terminal condition):

_____

_____

_____

(5) I particularly do not want the following kinds of life-sustaining treatment if I am diagnosed to have a terminal condition (you may list the specific types of life-sustaining treatment that you do not want if you have a terminal condition):

_____

_____

_____

(6) I recognize that if I reject artificially administered sustenance, then I may die of dehydration or malnutrition rather than from my illness or injury. The following are my feelings and wishes regarding artificially administered sustenance should I have a terminal condition (you may indicate whether you wish to receive food and fluids given to you in some other way than be mouth if you have a terminal condition):

_____

_____

_____

(7) Thoughts I feel are relevant to my instructions. (You may, but need not, give your religious beliefs, philosophy, or other personal values that you feel are important. You may also state preferences concerning the location of your care.):

_____

_____

_____

(8) **Proxy Designation.** (If you wish, you may name someone to see that your wishes are carried out, but you do not have to do this. You may also name a proxy without including specific instructions regarding your care. If you name a proxy, you should discuss your wishes with that person.)

If I become unable to communicate my instructions, I designate the following person(s) to act on my behalf consistently with my instructions, if any, as stated in this document. Unless I write instructions that limit my proxy's authority, my proxy has full power and authority to make health care decisions for me. If a guardian or conservator of the person is to be appointed for me, I nominate my proxy named in this document to act as guardian or conservator of my person.

Name:_____

Address:_____

Phone Number:_____

Relationship: (If any) _____

If the person I have named above refuses or is unable or unavailable to act on my behalf, or if I revoke that person's authority to act as my proxy, I authorize the following person to do so:

Name:_____

Address:_____

Phone Number:_____

Relationship: (If any) _____

I understand that I have the right to revoke the appointment of the persons named above to act on my behalf at any time by communicating that decision to the proxy or my health care provider.

(9) **Organ Donation After Death.** (If you wish, you may indicate whether you want to be an organ donor upon your death.) Initial the statement which expresses your wish:

_____ In the event of my death, I would like to donate my organs. I understand that to become an organ donor, I must be declared brain dead. My organ function may be maintained artificially on a breathing machine, (i.e., artificial ventilation), so that my organs can be removed.

Limitations or special wishes: (If any) _____

_____

_____

I understand that, upon my death, my next of kin may be asked permission for donation. Therefore, it is in my best interests to inform my next of kin about my decision ahead of time and ask them to honor my request.

I (have) (have not) agreed in another document or on another form to donate some or all of my organs when I die.

_____ I do not wish to become an organ donor upon my death.

DATE: _____   SIGNED: _____

STATE OF _____

COUNTY OF _____

Subscribed, sworn to, and acknowledged before me by _____ on this _____ day of _____, 19____.

_____

NOTARY PUBLIC

OR

(Sign and date here in the presence of two adult witnesses, neither of whom is entitled to any part of your estate under a will or by operation of law, and neither of whom is your proxy.)

I certify that the declarant voluntarily signed this living will in my presence and that the declarant is personally known to me. I am not named as a proxy by the living will, and to the best of my knowledge, I am not entitled to any part of the estate of the declarant under a will or by operation of law.

Witness _____   Address _____

_____

Witness _____   Address _____

_____

Reminder: Keep the signed original with your personal papers.
Give signed copies to your doctor, family, and proxy.

DECLARATION

DECLARATION made on _____, 19____ (date) by _____ (person's name) of _____ (address), _____ (Social Security Number).

I, _____, being of sound mind, declare that if at any time I should suffer a terminal physical condition which causes me severe distress or unconsciousness, and my physician, with the concurrence of two (2) other physicians, believes that there is no expectation of my regaining consciousness or a state of health that is meaningful to me and but for the use of life-sustaining mechanisms my death would be imminent, I desire that the mechanisms be withdrawn so that I may die naturally. However, if I have been diagnosed as pregnant and that diagnosis is known to my physician, this declaration shall have no force or effect during the course of my pregnancy. I further declare that this declaration shall be honored by my family as the final expression of my desires concerning the manner in which I die.

SIGNED: _____

I hereby witness this declaration and attest that:
    (1) I personally know the Declarant and believe the Declarant to be of sound mind.
    (2) To the best of my knowledge, at the time of the execution of this declaration, I:
        (a) Am not related to the Declarant by blood or marriage,
        (b) Do not have any claim on the estate of the Declarant,
        (c) Am not entitled to any portion of the Declarant's estate by any will or by operation of law, and
        (d) Am not a physician attending the Declarant or a person employed by a physician attending the Declarant.

WITNESS: _____
ADDRESS: _____
_____
SOCIAL SECURITY NUMBER: _____

WITNESS: _____
ADDRESS: _____
_____
SOCIAL SECURITY NUMBER: _____

THIS DECLARATION MUST BE FILED WITH THE BUREAU OF VITAL STATISTICS OF THE STATE BOARD OF HEALTH

DECLARATION

I have the primary right to make my own decisions concerning treatment that might unduly prolong the dying process. By this declaration I express to my physician, family and friends my intent. If I should have a terminal condition it is my desire that my dying not be prolonged by administration of death-prolonging procedures. If my condition is terminal and I am unable to participate in decisions regarding my medical treatment, I direct my attending physician to withhold or withdraw medical procedures that merely prolong the dying process and are not necessary to my comfort or to alleviate pain. It is not my intent to authorize affirmative or deliberate acts or omissions to shorten my life rather only to permit the natural process of dying.

Signed this _____ day of _____, 19_____.

Signature _____

City, County and State of residence_____

The declarant is known to me, is eighteen years of age or older, of sound mind and voluntarily signed this document in my presence.

Witness_____
Address_____
_____

Witness_____
Address_____
_____

REVOCATION PROVISION

I hereby revoke the above declaration,

Signed_____
(Signature of Declarant)

Date_____

Directive to Physicians

If I should have an incurable or irreversible condition that, without the administration of life-sustaining treatment, will, in the opinion of my attending physician, cause my death within a relatively short time and I am no longer able to make decisions regarding my medical treatment, I direct my attending physician, pursuant to the Montana Rights of the Terminally Ill Act, to withhold or withdraw treatment that only prolongs the process of dying and is not necessary to my comfort or to alleviate pain.

Signed this _____ day of _____, 19_____.
Signature_____
City, County, and State of Residence_____

The declarant voluntarily signed this document in my presence.

Witness_____
Address_____

Witness_____
Address_____

DECLARATION

If I should lapse into a persistent vegetative state or have an incurable and irreversible condition that, without the administration of life-sustaining treatment, will, in the opinion of my attending physician, cause my death within a relatively short time and I am no longer able to make decisions regarding my medical treatment, I direct my attending physician, pursuant to the Rights of the Terminally Ill Act, to withhold or withdraw life sustaining treatment that is not necessary for my comfort or to alleviate pain.

Signed this _____ day of _____.

Signature _____

Address _____

_____

The declarant voluntarily signed this writing in my presence.

_____   _____

Witness   Witness

_____   _____

Address   Address

_____   _____

Or

The declarant voluntarily signed this writing in my presence.

_____

Notary Public

DIRECTIVE REGARDING HEALTH CARE DECISIONS

WARNING TO PERSON EXECUTING THIS DOCUMENT

THIS IS AN IMPORTANT LEGAL DOCUMENT. BEFORE EXECUTING THIS DOCUMENT, YOU SHOULD KNOW THESE IMPORTANT FACTS:

1. NOTWITHSTANDING THIS DOCUMENT, YOU HAVE THE RIGHT TO MAKE MEDICAL AND OTHER HEALTH CARE DECISIONS FOR YOURSELF SO LONG AS YOU CAN GIVE INFORMED CONSENT WITH RESPECT TO THE PARTICULAR DECISION. IN ADDITION, NO TREATMENT MAY BE GIVEN TO YOU OVER YOUR OBJECTION, AND HEALTH CARE NECESSARY TO KEEP YOU ALIVE MAY NOT BE STOPPED IF YOU OBJECT.

2. IF THERE IS ANYTHING IN THIS DOCUMENT THAT YOU DO NOT UNDERSTAND, YOU SHOULD ASK A LAWYER TO EXPLAIN IT TO YOU.

STATEMENT OF DESIRES

(You can, but are not required to, indicate your desires below. If you wish to indicate your desires, you may INITIAL the statement or statements that reflect your desires and/or write your own statements in the space below.)

(If the statement reflects your desires, initial the box next to the statement.)

[   ]   1. I desire that my life be prolonged to the greatest extent possible, without regard to my condition, the chances I have for recovery or long-term survival, or the cost of the procedures.

[   ]   2. If I am in a coma which my doctors have reasonably concluded is irreversible, I desire that life-sustaining or prolonging treatments not be used. (Also should utilize provisions of NRS 449.535 to 449.690, inclusive, if this subparagraph is initialed.)

[   ]   3. If I have an incurable or terminal condition or illness and no reasonable hope of long term recovery or survival, desire that life sustaining or prolonging treatments not be used. (Also should utilize provisions of NRS 449.535 to 449.690, inclusive, if this subparagraph is initialed.)

[   ]   4. Withholding or withdrawal of artificial nutrition and hydration may result in death by starvation or dehydration. I want to receive or continue receiving artificial nutrition and hydration by way of the gastro-intestinal tract after all other treatment is withheld.

[   ]   5. I do not desire treatment to be provided and/or continued if the burdens of the treatment outweigh the expected benefits. This determination should consider the relief of suffering, the preservation or restoration or functioning, and the quality as well as the extent of the possible extension of my life.

(If you wish to change your answer, you may do so by drawing an "X" through the answer you do not want, and circling the answer you prefer.)

Other or Additional Statements of Desires:_____

_____

(THIS DOCUMENT WILL NOT BE VALID UNLESS IT IS EITHER (1) SIGNED BY AT LEAST TWO QUALIFIED WITNESSES WHO ARE PERSONALLY KNOWN TO YOU AND WHO ARE PRESENT WHEN YOU SIGN OR ACKNOWLEDGE YOUR SIGNATURE OR (2) ACKNOWLEDGED BEFORE A NOTARY PUBLIC.)

_____
(Your Signature)

CERTIFICATE OR ACKNOWLEDGMENT OF NOTARY PUBLIC

(You may use ACKNOWLEDGMENT before a notary public instead of the statement of witnesses.)

State of Nevada   )
) ss.
County of _____)

On this _____ day of _____, in the year _____, before me, _____ _____(here insert name of notary public) personally appeared _____ _____(here insert name of principal) personally known to me (or proved to me on the basis of satisfactory evidence) to be the person whose name is subscribed to this instrument, and acknowledged that he or she executed it. I declare under penalty or perjury that the person whose name is ascribed to this instrument appears to be of sound mind and under no duress, fraud, or undue influence.

NOTARY SEAL

_____
(Signature of Notary Public)

STATEMENT OF WITNESSES

(You should carefully read and follow this witnessing procedure. This document will not be valid unless you comply with the witnessing procedure. If you elect to use witnesses instead of having this document notarized you must use two qualified adult witnesses. None of the following may be used as a witness: (1) a person you designate as your attorney-in-fact to make health care decisions for you, (2) a provider of health care, (3) an employee of a provider of health care, (4) the operator of a health care facility, (5) an employee of an operator of a health care facility. At least one of the witnesses must make the additional declaration set out following the place where the witnesses sign.)

I declare under penalty of perjury that the principal is personally known to me, that the principal signed or acknowledged this living will in my presence, that the principal appears to be of sound mind and under no duress, fraud, or undue influence, that I am not the person appointed as attorney-in-fact to make health care decisions for the principal, and that I am not a provider of health care, an employee of a provider of health care, the operator of a community care facility, nor an employee of an operator of a health care facility.

Signature:_____   Signature:_____
Print Name:_____   Print Name:_____
Residence Address:_____   Residence Address:_____

_____   _____
Date:_____   Date:_____

(AT LEAST ONE OF THE ABOVE WITNESSES MUST ALSO SIGN THE FOLLOWING DECLARATION.)

I declare under penalty of perjury that I am not related to the principal by blood, marriage, or adoption, and to the best of my knowledge I am not entitled to any part of the estate of the principal upon the death or the principal under a will now existing or by operation of law.

Signature:_____
Print Name:_____
Residence Address:_____

_____
Date:_____

DECLARATION

Declaration made this _____ day of _____ (month, year). I, _____, being of sound mind, willfully and voluntarily make known my desire that my dying shall not be artificially prolonged under the circumstances set forth below, do hereby declare:

If at any time I should have an incurable injury, disease, or illness certified to be a terminal condition or a permanently unconscious condition by 2 physicians who have personally examined me, one of whom shall be my attending physician, and the physicians have determined that my death will occur whether or not life-sustaining procedures are utilized or that I will remain in a permanently unconscious condition and where the application of life-sustaining procedures would serve only to artificially prolong the dying process, I direct that such procedures be withheld or withdrawn, and that I be permitted to die naturally with only the administration of medication, sustenance, or the performance of any medical procedure deemed necessary to provide me with comfort care. I realize that situations could arise in which the only way to allow me to die would be to discontinue artificial nutrition and hydration. In carrying out any instruction I have given under this section, I authorize that artificial nutrition and hydration not be started or, if started, be discontinued.

(yes) (no) (Circle your choice and initial beneath it. If you choose "yes," artificial nutrition and _____ hydration will be provided and will not be removed.)

In the absence of my ability to give directions regarding the use of such life-sustaining procedures, it is my intention that this declaration shall be honored by my family and physicians as the final expression of my right to refuse medical or surgical treatment and accept the consequences of such refusal.

I understand the full import of this declaration, and I am emotionally and mentally competent to make this declaration.

Signed_____

State of _____
_____County

We, the following witnesses, being duly sworn each declare to the notary public or justice of the peace or other official signing below as follows:

1. The declarant signed the instrument as a free and voluntary act for the purposes expressed, or expressly directed another to sign for him.
2. Each witness signed at the request of the declarant, in his presence, and in the presence of the other witness.
3. To the best of my knowledge, at the time of the signing the declarant was at least 18 years of age, and was of sane mind and under no constraint or undue influence.

_____ Witness
_____ Witness

Sworn to and signed before me by _____, declarant, _____ and _____, witnesses on _____.

_____
Signature

_____
Official Capacity

OPTIONAL ADVANCE HEALTH-CARE DIRECTIVE

Explanation

You have the right to give instructions about your own health care. You also have the right to name someone else to make health-care decisions for you. This form lets you do either or both of these things. It also lets you express your wishes regarding the designation of your primary physician.

THIS FORM IS OPTIONAL. Each paragraph and word of this form is optional. If you use this form, you may strike, complete or modify all or any part of it. You are free to use a different form. You do not have to sign any form.

PART 1 of this form is a power of attorney for health care. Part 1 lets you name another individual as agent to make health-care decisions for you if you become incapable of making your own decisions or if you want someone else to make those decisions for you now even though you are still capable. You may also name an alternate agent to act for you if your first choice is not willing, able or reasonably available to make decisions for you. Unless related to you, your agent may not be an owner, operator or employee of a health-care institution at which you are receiving care.

Unless the form you sign limits the authority of your agent, your agent may make all health-care decisions for you. This form has a place for you to limit the authority of your agent. You need not limit the authority of your agent if you wish to rely on your agent for all health-care decisions that may have to be made. If you choose not to limit the authority of your agent, your agent will have the right to:

(a) consent or refuse consent to any care, treatment, service or procedure to maintain, diagnose or otherwise affect a physical or mental condition;

(b) select or discharge health-care providers and institutions;

(c) approve or disapprove diagnostic tests, surgical procedures, programs of medication and orders not to resuscitate; and

(d) direct the provision, withholding or withdrawal of artificial nutrition and hydration and all other forms of health care.

PART 2 of this form lets you give specific instructions about any aspect of your health care. Choices are provided for you to express your wishes regarding the provision, withholding or withdrawal of treatment to keep you alive, including the provision of artificial nutrition and hydration, as well as the provision of pain relief. Space is also provided for you to add to the choices you have made or for you to write out any additional wishes.

PART 3 of this form lets you designate a physician to have primary responsibility for your health care.

After completing this form, sign and date the form at the end. It is recommended but not required that you request two other individuals to sign as witnesses. Give a copy of the signed and completed form to your physician, to any other health-care providers you may have, to any health-care institution at which you are receiving care and to any health-care agents you have named. You should talk to the person you have named as agent to make sure that he or she understands your wishes and is willing to take the responsibility.

You have the right to revoke this advance health-care directive or replace this form at any time.

* * * * * * * * * * * * * * * * * * *

PART 1. POWER OF ATTORNEY FOR HEALTH CARE

(1) DESIGNATION OF AGENT: I designate the following individual as my agent to make health-care decisions for me:

_____
(name of individual you choose as agent)

_____
(address)   (city)   (state)   (zip code)

_____
(home phone)   (work phone)

If I revoke my agent's authority or if my agent is not willing, able or reasonably available to make a health-care decision for me, I designate as my first alternate agent:

_____
(name of individual you choose as first alternate agent)

_____
(address)   (city)   (state)   (zip code)

_____
(home phone)   (work phone)

If I revoke the authority of my agent and first alternate agent or if neither is willing, able or reasonably available to make a health-care decision for me, I designate as my second alternate agent:

_____
(name of individual you choose as second alternate agent)

_____
(address)   (city)   (state)   (zip code)

_____
(home phone)   (work phone)

(2) AGENT'S AUTHORITY: My agent is authorized to obtain and review medical records, reports and information about me and to make all health-care decisions for me, including decisions to provide, withhold or withdraw artificial nutrition, hydration and all other forms of health care to keep me alive, except as I state here:

_____
_____
_____
(Add additional sheets if needed.)

(3) WHEN AGENT'S AUTHORITY BECOMES EFFECTIVE: My agent's authority becomes effective when my primary physician and one other qualified health-care professional determine that I am unable to make my own health-care decisions, unless I mark the following box. If I mark this box [ ], my agent's authority to make health-care decisions for me takes effect immediately.

(4) AGENT'S OBLIGATIONS: My agent shall make health-care decisions for me in accordance with this power of attorney for health care, any instructions I give in Part 2 of this form and my other wishes to the extent known to my agent. To the extent my wishes are unknown, my agent shall make health-care decisions for me

in accordance with what my agent determines to be in my best interest. In determining my best interest, my agent shall consider my personal values to the extent known to my agent.

(5) NOMINATION OF GUARDIAN: If a guardian of my person needs to be appointed for me by a court, I nominate the agent designated in this form. If that agent is not willing, able or reasonably available to act as guardian, I nominate the alternate agents whom I have named, in the order designated.

PART 2. INSTRUCTIONS FOR HEALTH CARE

If you are satisfied to allow your agent to determine what is best for you in making end-of-life decisions, you need not fill out this part of the form. If you do fill out this part of the form, you may strike any wording you do not want.

(6) END-OF-LIFE DECISIONS: I direct that my health-care providers and others involved in my care provide, withhold or withdraw treatment in accordance with the choice I have marked below:

[　](a)　Choice Not To Prolong Life: I do not want my life to be prolonged if (i) I have an incurable and irreversible condition that will result in my death within a relatively short time, (ii) I become unconscious and, to a reasonable degree of medical certainty, I will not regain consciousness or (iii) the likely risks and burdens of treatment would outweigh the expected benefits, OR

[　](b)　Choice To Prolong Life: I want my life to be prolonged as long as possible within the limits of generally accepted health-care standards.

(7) ARTIFICIAL NUTRITION AND HYDRATION: If I have selected the above choice NOT to prolong life under specified conditions, I also specify that I _____ do or _____ do not want artificial nutrition and hydration provided to me.

(8) RELIEF FROM PAIN: Except as I state in the following space, I direct that treatment for easing pain or discomfort be provided at all times, even if it hastens my death: _____
_____
_____
_____

(Add additional sheets if needed.)

PART 3. PRIMARY PHYSICIAN

(10)　　I designate the following physician as my primary physician:

_____
(name of physician)　　　　　　　　　　　　　　　　　　　　　　　　(phone)

_____
(address)　　　　　　　　　　　　(city)　　　　　　　(state)　　　　　　(zip code)

If the physician I have designated above is not willing, able or reasonably available to act as my primary physician, I designate the following physician as my primary physician:

_____
(name of physician)　　　　　　　　　　　　　　　　　　　　　　　　(phone)

_____
(address)　　　　　　　　　　　　(city)　　　　　　　(state)　　　　　　(zip code)

* * * * * * * * * * * * * * * * * * * *

(11)　　EFFECT OF COPY: A copy of this form has the same effect as the original.

(12)   REVOCATION: I understand that I may revoke this OPTIONAL ADVANCE HEALTH-CARE DIRECTIVE at any time, and that if I revoke it, I should promptly notify my supervising health-care provider and any health-care institution where I am receiving care and any others to whom I have given copies of this power of attorney. I understand that I may revoke the designation of an agent only by a signed writing or by personally informing the supervising health-care provider.

(13)   SIGNATURES: Sign and date the form here:

_____
(date)

_____
(address)

_____
(city)   (state)

_____
(sign your name)

_____
(print your name)

_____
(your social security number)

(Optional) SIGNATURE OF WITNESSES:

First witness

_____
(print name)

_____
(address)

_____
(city)   (state)

_____
(signature of witness)

_____
(date)

Second witness

_____
(print name)

_____
(address)

_____
(city)   (state)

_____
(signature of witness)

_____
(date)

Declaration Of A Desire For A Natural Death

I, _____, being of sound mind, desire that, as specified below, my life not be prolonged by extraordinary means or be artificial nutrition or hydration if my condition is determined to be terminal and incurable or if I am diagnosed as being in a persistent vegetative state. I am aware and understand that this writing authorizes a physician to withhold or discontinue extraordinary means or artificial nutrition or hydration, in accordance with my specifications set forth below:

(Initial any of the following, as desired):

_____ If my condition is determined to be terminal and incurable, I authorize the following:

        _____ My physician may withhold or discontinue extraordinary means only.

        _____ In addition to withholding or discontinuing extraordinary means if such means are necessary, my physician may withhold or discontinue either artificial nutrition or hydration, or both.

_____ If my physician determines that I am in a persistent vegetative state, I authorize the following:

        _____ My physician may withhold or discontinue extraordinary means only.

        _____ In addition to withholding or discontinuing extraordinary means if such means are necessary, my physician may withhold or discontinue either artificial nutrition or hydration, or both.

This the _____ day of _____, _____.

Signature _____

I hereby state that the declarant, _____, being of sound mind signed the above declaration in my presence and that I am not related to the declarant by blood or marriage and that I do not know or have a reasonable expectation that I would be entitled to any portion of the estate of the declarant under any existing will or codicil of the declarant or as an heir under the Intestate Succession Act if the declarant died on this date without a will. I also state that I am not the declarant's attending physician or an employee of the declarant's attending physician, or an employee of a health facility in which the declarant is a patient or an employee of a nursing home or any group-care home where the declarant resides. I further state that I do not now have any claim against the declarant.

Witness _____

Witness _____

The clerk or assistant clerk, of a notary public may, upon proper proof, certify the declaration as follows:

Certificate

I, _____, Clerk (Assistant Clerk) of Superior Court or Notary Public (circle one as appropriate) for _____ County hereby certify that _____, the declarant, appeared before me and swore to me and to the witnesses in my presence that this instrument is his Declaration Of A Desire For A Natural Death, and that he had willingly and voluntarily made and executed it as his free act and deed for the purposes expressed in it.

I further certify that _____ and _____, witnesses, appeared before me and swore that they witnessed _____, declarant, sign the attached declaration, believing him to be of sound mind; and also swore that at the time they witnessed the declaration (i) they were not related within the third degree to the declarant or to the declarant's spouse, and (ii) they did not know or have a reasonable expectation that they would be entitled to any portion of the estate of the declarant under any existing will of the declarant or codicil thereto then existing or under the Intestate Succession Act as it provided at that time, and (iii) they were not a physician attending the declarant or an employee of an attending physician or an employee of a health facility in which the declarant was a patient or an employee of a nursing home or any group-care home in which the declarant resided, and (iv) they did not have a claim against the declarant. I further certify that I am satisfied as to the genuineness and due execution of the declaration.

This the _____ day of _____, _____.

_____
Clerk (Assistant Clerk) of Superior Court or Notary Public (circle one as appropriate) for the County of _____

Advance Directive for Health Care

I,_____, being of sound mind and eighteen (18) years of age or older, willfully and voluntarily make known my desire, by my instructions to others through my living will, or by my appointment of a health care proxy, or both, that my life shall not be artificially prolonged under the circumstances set forth below. I thus do hereby declare:

I. Living Will

a. If my attending physician and another physician determine that I am no longer able to make decisions regarding my medical treatment, I direct my attending physician and other health care providers, pursuant to the Oklahoma Rights of the Terminally Ill or Persistently Unconscious Act, to withhold or withdraw treatment from me under the circumstances I have indicated below by my signature. I understand that I will be given treatment that is necessary for my comfort or to alleviate my pain.

b. If I have a terminal condition:

    (1) I direct that life-sustaining treatment shall be withheld or withdrawn if such treatment would only prolong my process of dying, and if my attending physician and another physician determine that I have an incurable and irreversible condition that even with the administration of life-sustaining treatment will cause my death within six (6) months.

    _____(signature)

    (2) I understand that the subject of the artificial administration of nutrition and hydration (food and water) that will only prolong the process of dying from an incurable and irreversible condition is of particular importance. I understand that if I do not sign this paragraph, artificially administered nutrition and hydration will be administered to me. I further understand that if I sign this paragraph, I am authorizing the withholding or withdrawal of artificially administered nutrition (food) and hydration (water).

    _____(signature)

    (3) I direct that (add other medical directives, if any)_____
    _____
    _____

    _____ (signature)

c. If I am persistently unconscious:

    (1) I direct that life-sustaining treatment be withheld or withdrawn if such treatment will only serve to maintain me in an irreversible condition, as determined by my attending physician and another physician, in which thought and awareness of self and environment are absent.

    _____(signature)

    (2) I understand that the subject of the artificial administration of nutrition and hydration (food and water) for individuals who have become persistently unconscious is of particular importance. I understand that if I do not sign this paragraph, artificially administered nutrition and hydration will be

administered to me. I further understand that if I sign this paragraph, I am authorizing the withholding or withdrawal of artificially administered nutrition (food) and hydration (water).

_____(signature)

(3) I direct that (add other medical directives, if any)_____
_____
_____

_____(signature)

II. My Appointment of My Health Care Proxy

a. If my attending physician and another physician determine that I am no longer able to make decisions regarding my medical treatment, I direct my attending physician and other health care providers pursuant to the Oklahoma Rights of the Terminally Ill or Persistently Unconscious Act to follow the instructions of _____, whom I appoint as my health care proxy. If my health care proxy is unable or unwilling to serve, I appoint _____as my alternate health care proxy with the same authority. My health care proxy is authorized to make whatever medical treatment decisions I could make if I were able, except that decisions regarding life-sustaining treatment can be made by my health care proxy or alternate health care proxy only as I indicate in the following sections.

b. If I have a terminal condition:

(1) I authorize my health care proxy to direct that life-sustaining treatment be withheld or withdrawn if such treatment would only prolong my process of dying and if my attending physician and another physician determine that I have an incurable and irreversible condition that even with the administration of life-sustaining treatment will cause my death within six (6) months.

_____(signature)

(2) I understand that the subject of the artificial administration of nutrition and hydration (food and water) is of particular importance. I understand that if I do not sign this paragraph, artificially administered nutrition (food) or hydration (water) will be administered to me. I further understand that if I sign this paragraph, I am authorizing the withholding or withdrawal of artificially administered nutrition and hydration.

_____(signature)

(3) I authorize my health care proxy to (add other medical directives, if any)_____
_____
_____

_____(signature)

c. If I am persistently unconscious:

(1) I authorize my health care proxy to direct that life-sustaining treatment be withheld or withdrawn if such treatment will only serve to maintain me in an irreversible condition, as determined by my

attending physician and another physician, in which thought and awareness of self and environment are absent.

_____(signature)

(2) I understand that the subject of the artificial administration of nutrition and hydration (food and water) is of particular importance. I understand that if I do not sign this paragraph, artificially administered nutrition (food) and hydration (water) will be administered to me. I further understand that if I sign this paragraph, I am authorizing the withholding and withdrawal of artificially administered nutrition and hydration.

_____ (signature)

(3) I authorize my health care proxy to (add other medical directives, if any)_____
_____
_____

_____(signature)

III. Anatomical Gifts

I direct that at the time of my death my entire body or designated body organs or body parts be donated for purposes of transplantation, therapy, advancement or medical or dental science or research or education pursuant to the provisions of the Uniform Anatomical Gift Act. Death means either irreversible cessation of circulatory and respiratory functions or irreversible cessation of all functions of the entire brain, including the brain stem. I specifically donate:

[ ] My entire body; or
[ ] The following body organs or parts:

( ) lungs,	( ) liver,	( ) pancreas,	( ) heart,	( ) kidneys,
( ) brain,	( ) skin,	( ) bones/marrow,	( ) bloods/fluids,	( ) tissue,
( ) arteries,	( ) eyes/cornea/lens,	( ) glands,	( ) other: _____	

_____(signature)

IV. Conflicting Provisions

I understand that if I have completed both a living will and have appointed a health care proxy, and if there is a conflict between my health care proxy's decision and my living will, my living will shall take precedence unless I indicate otherwise. _____

_____(signature)

V. General Provisions

a. I understand that if I have been diagnosed as pregnant and that diagnosis is known to my attending physician, this advance directive shall have no force or effect during the course of my pregnancy.
b. In the absence of my ability to give directions regarding the use of life-sustaining procedures, it is my intention that this advance directive shall be honored by my family and physicians as the final expression of my legal right to refuse medical or surgical treatment including, but not limited to, the administration of any life-sustaining procedures, and I accept the consequences of such refusal.
c. This advance directive shall be in effect until it is revoked.

d. I understand that I may revoke this advance directive at any time.
e. I understand and agree that if I have any prior directives, and, if I sign this advance directive, my prior directives are revoked.
f. I understand the full importance of this advance directive and I am emotionally and mentally competent to make this advance directive.

Signed this _____ day of _____ , 19_____.

_____
(Signature)

_____
City, County and State of Residence

This advance directive was signed in my presence.

_____   _____
(Signature of Witness)   (Signature of Witness)

_____   _____
(Address)   (Address)

ADVANCE DIRECTIVE

YOU DO NOT HAVE TO FILL OUT AND SIGN THIS FORM
PART A: IMPORTANT INFORMATION ABOUT THIS ADVANCE DIRECTIVE

This is an important legal document. It can control critical decisions about your health care. Before signing, consider these important facts:

Facts About Part B (Appointing a Health Care Representative)

You have the right to name a person to direct your health care when you cannot do so. This person is called your "health care representative." You can do this by using Part B of this form. Your representative must accept on Part E of this form.

You can write in this document any restrictions you want on how your representative will make decisions for you. Your representative must follow your desires as stated in this document or otherwise made known. If your desires are unknown, your representative must try to act in your best interest. Your representative can resign at any time.

Facts About Part C (Giving Health Care Instructions)

You also have the right to give instructions for health care providers to follow if you become unable to direct your care. You can do this by using Part C of this form.

Facts About Completing This Form

This form is valid only if you sign it voluntarily and when you are of sound mind. If you do not want an advance directive, you do not have to sign this form.

Unless you have limited the duration of this advance directive, it will not expire. If you have set an expiration date, and you become unable to direct your health care before that date, this advance directive will not expire until you are able to make those decisions again.

You may revoke this document at any time. To do so, notify your representative and your health care provider of the revocation.

Despite this document, you have the right to decide your own health care as long as you are able to do so.

If there is anything in this document that you do not understand, ask a lawyer to explain it to you.

You may sign PART B, PART C, or both parts. You may cross out words that don't express your wishes or add words that better express your wishes. Witnesses must sign PART D.

Print your NAME, BIRTHDATE AND ADDRESS here:

_____   _____
(Name)   (Birthdate)

_____
(Address)

Unless revoked or suspended, this advance directive will continue for:
INITIAL ONE:
_____ My entire life
_____ Other period (_____ Years)

PART B: APPOINTMENT OF HEALTH CARE REPRESENTATIVE

I appoint _____ as my health care representative.
My representative's address is_____,
and telephone number is_____.
I appoint_____ as my alternate health care representative. My alternate's address is_____,
and telephone number is_____.

I authorize my representative (or alternate) to direct my health care when I can't do so.

NOTE: You may not appoint your doctor, an employee of your doctor, or an owner, operator or employee of your health care facility, unless that person is related to you by blood, marriage or adoption or that person was appointed before your admission into the health care facility.

1. Limits.
   Special Conditions or Instructions:

   _____
   _____
   _____

   INITIAL IF THIS APPLIES: _____ I have executed a Health Care Instruction or Directive to Physicians. My representative is to honor it.

2. Life Support. "Life support" refers to any medical means for maintaining life, including procedures, devices and medications. If you refuse life support, you will still get routine measures to keep you clean and comfortable.
   INITIAL IF THIS APPLIES: _____ My representative MAY decide about life support for me. (If you don't initial this space, then your representative MAY NOT decide about life support.)

3. Tube Feeding. One sort of life support is food and water supplied artificially by medical device, known as tube feeding.
   INITIAL IF THIS APPLIES: _____ My representative MAY decide about tube feeding for me. (If you don't initial this space, then your representative MAY NOT decide about tube feeding.)

SIGN HERE TO APPOINT A HEALTH CARE REPRESENTATIVE

_____   _____
(Signature of person making appointment)   (Date)

PART C: HEALTH CARE INSTRUCTIONS

NOTE: In filling out these instructions, keep the following in mind:
- The term "as my physician recommends" means that you want your physician to try life support if your physician believes it could be helpful and then discontinue it if it is not helping your health condition or symptoms.
- "Life support" and "tube feeding" are defined in Part B above.
- If you refuse tube feeding, you should understand that malnutrition, dehydration and death will probably result.
- You will get care for your comfort and cleanliness, no matter what choices you make.
- You may either give specific instructions by filling out Items 1 to 4 below, or you may use the general instruction provided by Item 5.

Here are my desires about my health care if my doctor and another knowledgeable doctor confirm that I am in a medical condition described below:

1. Close to Death. If I am close to death and life support would only postpone the moment of my death:
A. INITIAL ONE: B. INITIAL ONE:
   _____ I want to receive tube feeding.   _____ I want any other life support that may apply.

   _____ I want tube feeding only as my   _____ I want life support only as my physician recommends.
          physician recommends.   recommends.
   _____ I DO NOT WANT tube feeding.   _____ I want NO life support.

2. <u>Permanently Unconscious.</u> If I am unconscious and it is very unlikely that I will ever become conscious again:

A. INITIAL ONE:

_____ I want to receive tube feeding.

_____ I want tube feeding only as my physician recommends.

_____ I DO NOT WANT tube feeding.

B. INITIAL ONE:

_____ I want any other life support that may apply.

_____ I want life support only as my physician recommends.

_____ I want NO life support.

3. **Advanced Progressive Illness.** If I have a progressive illness that will be fatal and is in an advanced stage, and I am consistently and permanently unable to communicate by any means, swallow food and water safely, care for myself and recognize my family and other people, and it is very unlikely that my condition will substantially improve:

A. INITIAL ONE:

_____ I want to receive tube feeding.

_____ I want tube feeding only as my physician recommends.

_____ I DO NOT WANT tube feeding.

B. INITIAL ONE:

_____ I want any other life support that may apply.

_____ I want life support only as my physician recommends.

_____ I want NO life support.

4. <u>Extraordinary Suffering.</u> If life support would not help my medical condition and would make me suffer permanent and severe pain:

A. INITIAL ONE:

_____ I want to receive tube feeding.

_____ I want tube feeding only as my physician recommends.

_____ I DO NOT WANT tube feeding.

B. INITIAL ONE:

_____ I want any other life support that may apply.

_____ I want life support only as my physician recommends.

_____ I want NO life support.

5. <u>General Instruction.</u>

INITIAL IF THIS APPLIES: _____ I do not want my life to be prolonged by life support. I also do not want tube feeding as life support. I want my doctors to allow me to die naturally if my doctor and another knowledgeable doctor confirm I am in any of the medical conditions listed in Items 1 to 4 above.

6. <u>Additional Conditions or Instructions.</u>

_____

_____

_____

(Insert description of what you want done.)

7. <u>Other Documents.</u> A "health care power of attorney" is any document you may have signed to appoint a representative to make health care decisions for you.

INITIAL ONE: _____ I have previously signed a health care power of attorney. I want it to remain in effect unless I appointed a health care representative after signing the health care power of attorney.

_____ I have a health care power of attorney, and I REVOKE IT.

_____ I DO NOT have a health care power of attorney.

SIGN HERE TO GIVE INSTRUCTIONS

_____   _____

(Signature)   (Date)

PART D: DECLARATION OF WITNESSES

We declare that the person signing this advance directive:
(a) Is personally known to us or has provided proof of identity;
(b) Signed or acknowledged that person's signature on this advance directive in our presence;
(c) Appears to be of sound mind and not under duress, fraud or undue influence;
(d) Has not appointed either of us as health care representative or alternate representative; and
(e) Is not a patient for whom either of us is attending physician.

Witnessed By:

_____   _____
(Signature of Witness/Date)   (Printed Name of Witness)

_____   _____
(Signature of Witness/Date)   (Printed Name of Witness)

NOTE: One witness must not be a relative (by blood, marriage or adoption) of the person signing this advance directive. That witness must also not be entitled to any portion of the person's estate upon death. That witness must also not own, operate or be employed at a health care facility where the person is a patient or resident.

PART E: ACCEPTANCE BY HEALTH CARE REPRESENTATIVE

I accept this appointment and agree to serve as health care representative. I understand I must act consistently with the desires of the person I represent, as expressed in this advance directive or otherwise made known to me. If I do not know the desires of the person I represent, I have a duty to act in what I believe in good faith to be that person's best interest. I understand that this document allows me to decide about that person's health care only while that person cannot do so. I understand that the person who appointed me may revoke this appointment. If I learn that this document has been suspended or revoked, I will inform the person's current health care provider if known to me.

_____   _____
(Signature of Health Care Representative/Date)   (Signature of Alternate Health Care Representative/Date)

_____   _____
(Printed name)   (Printed name)

DECLARATION

I, _____, being of sound mind willfully and voluntarily make known my desire that my dying shall not be artificially prolonged under the circumstances set forth below, do hereby declare:

If I should have an incurable or irreversible condition that will cause my death within a relatively short time, and if I am unable to make decisions regarding my medical treatment, I direct my attending physician to withhold or withdraw procedures that merely prolong the dying process and are not necessary to my comfort, or to alleviate pain.

This authorization includes (   ) does not include (   ) the withholding or withdrawal of artificial feeding (check only one box above).

Signed this _____ day of _____, 19_____.

_____
Signature

_____

_____
Address

The declarant is personally known to me and voluntarily signed this document in my presence.

_____   _____
Witness   Witness

_____   _____

_____   _____
Address   Address

STATE OF SOUTH CAROLINA
COUNTY OF_____

DECLARATION
OF A DESIRE FOR A
NATURAL DEATH

I,_____, Declarant, being at least eighteen years of age and a resident of and domiciled in the City of_____ , County of_____, State of South Carolina, make this Declaration this ___ day of_____, 19_____.

I wilfully and voluntarily make known my desire that no life-sustaining procedures be used to prolong my dying if my condition is terminal or if I am in a state of permanent unconsciousness, and I declare:

If at any time I have a condition certified to be a terminal condition by two physicians who have personally examined me, one of whom is my attending physician, and the physicians have determined that my death could occur within a reasonably short period of time without the use of life-sustaining procedures or if the physicians certify that I am in a state of permanent unconsciousness and where the application of life-sustaining procedures would serve only to prolong the dying process, I direct that the procedures be withheld or withdrawn, and that I be permitted to die naturally with only the administration of medication or the performance of any medical procedure necessary to provide me with comfort care.

INSTRUCTIONS CONCERNING ARTIFICIAL NUTRITION AND HYDRATION

INITIAL ONE OF THE FOLLOWING STATEMENTS

If my condition is terminal and could result in death within a reasonably short time,
_____ I direct that nutrition and hydration BE PROVIDED through any medically indicated means, including medically or surgically implanted tubes.
_____ I direct that nutrition and hydration NOT BE PROVIDED through any medically indicated means, including medically or surgically implanted tubes.

INITIAL ONE OF THE FOLLOWING STATEMENTS

If I am in a persistent vegetative state or other condition of permanent unconsciousness,
_____ I direct that nutrition and hydration BE PROVIDED through any medically indicated means, including medically or surgically implanted tubes.
_____ I direct that nutrition and hydration NOT BE PROVIDED through any medically indicated means, including medically or surgically implanted tubes.

In the absence of my ability to give directions regarding the use of life-sustaining procedures, it is my intention that this Declaration be honored by my family and physicians and any health facility in which I may be a patient as the final expression of my legal right to refuse medical or surgical treatment, and I accept the consequences from the refusal.

I am aware that this Declaration authorizes a physician to withhold or withdraw life-sustaining procedures. I am emotionally and mentally competent to make this Declaration.

APPOINTMENT OF AN AGENT (OPTIONAL)

1. You may give another person authority to revoke this declaration on your behalf. If you wish to do so, please enter that person's name in the space below.
Name of Agent with Power to Revoke:_____
Address:_____
Telephone Number:_____
2. You may give another person authority to enforce this declaration on your behalf. If you wish to do so, please enter that person's name in the space below.
Name of Agent with Power to Enforce: _____
Address:_____
Telephone Number:_____

REVOCATION PROCEDURES

THIS DECLARATION MAY BE REVOKED BY ANY ONE OF THE FOLLOWING METHODS. HOWEVER, A REVOCATION IS NOT EFFECTIVE UNTIL IT IS COMMUNICATED TO THE ATTENDING PHYSICIAN.

(1) BY BEING DEFACED, TORN, OBLITERATED, OR OTHERWISE DESTROYED, IN EXPRESSION OF YOUR INTENT TO REVOKE, BY YOU OR BY SOME PERSON IN YOUR PRESENCE AND BY YOUR DIRECTION. REVOCATION BY DESTRUCTION OF ONE OR MORE OF MULTIPLE ORIGINAL DECLARATIONS REVOKES ALL OF THE ORIGINAL DECLARATIONS;

(2) BY A WRITTEN REVOCATION SIGNED AND DATED BY YOU EXPRESSING YOUR INTENT TO REVOKE;

(3) BY YOUR ORAL EXPRESSION OF YOUR INTENT TO REVOKE THE DECLARATION. AN ORAL REVOCATION COMMUNICATED TO THE ATTENDING PHYSICIAN BY A PERSON OTHER THAN YOU IS EFFECTIVE ONLY IF:

    (a) THE PERSON WAS PRESENT WHEN THE ORAL REVOCATION WAS MADE;

    (b) THE REVOCATION WAS COMMUNICATED TO THE PHYSICIAN WITHIN A REA-SONABLE TIME;

    (c) YOUR PHYSICAL OR MENTAL CONDITION MAKES IT IMPOSSIBLE FOR THE PHYSICIAN TO CONFIRM THROUGH SUBSEQUENT CONVERSATION WITH YOU THAT THE REVOCATION HAS OCCURRED.

TO BE EFFECTIVE AS A REVOCATION, THE ORAL EXPRESSION CLEARLY MUST INDI-CATE YOUR DESIRE THAT THE DECLARATION NOT BE GIVEN EFFECT OR THAT LIFE-SUSTAINING PROCEDURES BE ADMINISTERED;

(4) IF YOU, IN THE SPACE ABOVE, HAVE AUTHORIZED AN AGENT TO REVOKE THE DEC-LARATION, THE AGENT MAY REVOKE ORALLY OR BY A WRITTEN, SIGNED, AND DATED INSTRU-MENT. AN AGENT MAY REVOKE ONLY IF YOU ARE INCOMPETENT TO DO SO. AN AGENT MAY REVOKE THE DECLARATION PERMANENTLY OR TEMPORARILY.

(5) BY YOUR EXECUTING ANOTHER DECLARATION AT A LATER TIME.

_____

Signature of Declarant

STATE OF _____   AFFIDAVIT

COUNTY OF _____

We,_____and_____, The under-signed witnesses to the foregoing Declaration, dated the _____ day of_____, 19_____, at least one of being first duly sworn, declare to the undersigned authority, on the basis of our best information and belief, that the Declaration was on that date signed by the declarant as and for his DECLA-RATION OF A DESIRE FOR A NATURAL DEATH in our presence and we, at his request and in his pres-ence, and in the presence of each other subscribe our names as witnesses on that date. The declarant is personally known to us, and we believe him to be of sound mind. Each of us affirms that he is qualified as a witness to this Declaration under the provisions of the South Carolina Death With Dignity Act in that he is not related to the declarant by blood, marriage, or adoption, either as a spouse, lineal ancestor, descendant of the parents of the declarant, or spouse of any of them; nor directly financially responsible for the declarant's medical care; nor entitled to any portion of the declarant's estate upon his decease, whether under any will or as an heir by intestate succession, nor the beneficiary of a life insurance policy of the declarant; nor the declar-ant's attending physician; nor an employee of the attending physician; nor a person who has a claim against the declarant's decedent's estate as of this time. No more than one of us is an employee of a health facility in which the declarant is a patient. If the declarant is a resident in a hospital or nursing care facility at the date of exe-cution of this Declaration, at least one of us is an ombudsman designated by the State Ombudsman, Office of the Governor.

_____   _____

Witness   Witness

Subscribed before me by _____, the declarant, and sub-scribed and sworn to before me by_____, the witnesses, this _____ day of _____, 19 _____ .

_____

Signature

Notary Public for_____

My commission expires:_____

LIVING WILL DECLARATION

This is an important legal document. This document directs the medical treatment you are to receive in the event you are unable to participate in your own medical decisions and you are in a terminal condition. This document may state what kind of treatment you want or do not want to receive. This document can control whether you live or die. Prepare this document carefully. If you use this form, read it completely. You may want to seek professional help to make sure the form does what you intend and is completed without mistakes.

This document will remain valid and in effect until and unless you revoke it. Review this document periodically to make sure it continues to reflect your wishes. You may amend or revoke this document at any time by notifying your physician and other health-care providers. You should give copies of this Document to your physician and your family. This form is entirely optional. If you choose to use this form, please note that the form provides signature lines for you, the two witnesses whom you have selected and a notary public.

TO MY FAMILY, PHYSICIANS, AND ALL THOSE CONCERNED WITH MY CARE:

I,_____ willfully and voluntarily make this declaration as a directive to be followed if I am in a terminal condition and become unable to participate in decisions regarding my medical care.

With respect to any life-sustaining treatment, I direct the following:

(Initial only one of the following optional directives if you agree. If you do not agree with any of the following directives, space is provided below for you to write your own directives).

_____ NO LIFE-SUSTAINING TREATMENT. I direct that no life-sustaining treatment be provided. If life-sustaining treatment is begun, terminate it.

_____ TREATMENT FOR RESTORATION. Provide life-sustaining treatment only if and for so long as you believe treatment offers a reasonable possibility of restoring to me the ability to think and act for myself.

_____ TREAT UNLESS PERMANENTLY UNCONSCIOUS. If you believe that I am permanently unconscious and are satisfied that this condition is irreversible, then do not provide me with life-sustaining treatment, and if life-sustaining treatment is being provided to me, terminate it. If and so long as you believe that treatment has a reasonable possibility of restoring consciousness to me, then provide life-sustaining treatment.

_____ MAXIMUM TREATMENT. Preserve my life as long as possible, but do not provide treatment that is not in accordance with accepted medical standards as then in effect. (Artificial nutrition and hydration is food and water provided by means of a nasogastric tube or tubes inserted into the stomach, intestines, or veins. If you do not wish to receive this form of treatment, you must initial the statement below which reads: "I intend to include this treatment, among the 'life-sustaining treatment' that may be withheld or withdrawn.")

With respect to artificial nutrition and hydration, I wish to make clear that (Initial only one)

_____ I intend to include this treatment among the "life-sustaining treatment" that may be withheld or withdrawn.

_____ I do not intend to include this treatment among the "life-sustaining treatment" that may be withheld or withdrawn.

(If you do not agree with any of the printed directives and want to write your own, or if you want to write directives in addition to the printed provisions, or if you want to express some of your other thoughts, you can do so here.)

_____

_____

_____

Date:_____   _____

                                     (your signature)

_____   _____

(your address)   (type or print your signature)

The declarant voluntarily signed this document in my presence.

Witness _____   Witness_____

Address _____   Address _____

On this _____ day of_____, 19_____, the declarant, _____, and witnesses _____, and_____, personally appeared before the undersigned officer and signed the foregoing instrument in my presence. Dated this _____ day of _____, 19_____.

_____
Notary Public
My commission expires: _____

LIVING WILL

I, _____, willfully and voluntarily make known my desire that my dying shall not be artificially prolonged under the circumstances set forth below, and do hereby declare:

If at any time I should have a terminal condition and my attending physician has determined there is no reasonable medical expectation of recovery and which, as a medical probability, will result in my death, regardless of the use or discontinuance of medical treatment implemented for the purpose of sustaining life, or the life process, I direct that medical care be withheld or withdrawn, and that I be permitted to die naturally with only the administration of medications or the performance of any medical procedure deemed necessary to provide me with comfortable care or to alleviate pain.

By checking the appropriate line below, I specifically:

_____Authorize the withholding or withdrawal of artificially provided food, water or other nourishment or fluids.

_____DO NOT authorize the withholding or withdrawal of artificially provided food, water or other nourishment or fluids.

ORGAN DONOR CERTIFICATION:

Notwithstanding my previous declaration relative to the withholding or withdrawal of life-prolonging procedures, if as indicated below I have expressed my desire to donate my organs and/or tissues for transplantation, or any of them as specifically designated herein, I do direct my attending physician, if I have been determined dead according to Tennessee Code Annotated, § 68-3-501(b), to maintain me on artificial support systems only for the period of time required to maintain the viability of and to remove such organs and/or tissues.

By checking the appropriate line below, I specifically:

_____Desire to donate my organs and/or tissues for transplantation.

_____Desire to donate my _____
(insert specific organs and/or tissues for transplantation)

_____DO NOT desire to donate my organs or tissues for transplantation.

In the absence of my ability to give directions regarding my medical care, it is my intention that this declaration shall be honored by my family and physician as the final expression of my legal right to refuse medical care and accept the consequences of such refusal.

The definitions of terms used herein shall be as set forth in the Tennessee Right to Natural Death Act, Tennessee Code Annotated, § 32-11-103.

I understand the full import of this declaration, and I am emotionally and mentally competent to make this declaration.

In acknowledgment whereof, I do hereinafter affix my signature on this the _____ day of _____, 19_____.

_____
Declarant

We, the subscribing witnesses hereto, are personally acquainted with and subscribe our names hereto at the request of the declarant, an adult, whom we believe to be of sound mind, fully aware of the action taken herein and its possible consequence.

We, the undersigned witnesses, further declare that we are not related to the declarant by blood or marriage; that we are not entitled to any portion of the estate of the declarant upon the declarant's decease under any will or codicil thereto presently existing or by operation of law then existing; that we are not the attending physician, an employee of the attending physician or, health facility in which the declarant is a patient; and that we are not persons who, at the present time, have a claim against any portion of the estate of the declarant upon the declarant's death.

_____   _____
Witness   Witness

STATE OF TENNESSEE
COUNTY OF _____

Subscribed, sworn to and acknowledged before me by _____, the declarant, and subscribed and sworn to before me by _____ and _____, witnesses, this _____ day of _____, 19_____.

_____
Notary Public

My Commission Expires:_____

DIRECTIVE TO PHYSICIANS

Directive made this _____ day of _____ (month, year).

I _____, being of sound mind, wilfully and voluntarily make known my desire that my life shall not be artificially prolonged under the circumstances set forth in this directive.

1. If at any time I should have an incurable or irreversible condition caused by injury, disease, or illness certified to be a terminal condition by two physicians, and if the application of life-sustaining procedures would serve only to artificially postpone the moment of my death, and if my attending physician determines that my death is imminent or will result within a relatively short time without the application of life-sustaining procedures, I direct that those procedures be withheld or withdrawn, and that I be permitted to die naturally.

2. In the absence of my ability to give directions regarding the use of those life-sustaining procedures, it is my intention that this directive be honored by my family and physicians as the final expression of my legal right to refuse medical or surgical treatment and accept the consequences from that refusal.

3. If I have been diagnosed as pregnant and that diagnosis is known to my physician, this directive has no effect during my pregnancy.

4. This directive is in effect until it is revoked.

5. I understand the full import of this directive and I am emotionally and mentally competent to make this directive.

6. I understand that I may revoke this directive at any time.

Signed_____

_____
(City, County, and State of Residence)

I am not related to the declarant by blood or marriage. I would not be entitled to any portion of the declarant's estate on the declarant's death. I am not the attending physician or the declarant or an employee of the attending physician. I am not a patient in the heath care facility in which the declarant is a patient. I have no claim against any portion of the declarant's estate on the declarant's death. Furthermore, if I am an employee of a health care facility in which the declarant is a patient, I am not involved in the financial affairs of the health facility.

Witness _____

Witness _____

DIRECTIVE TO PHYSICIANS AND PROVIDERS OF MEDICAL SERVICES

(Pursuant to Section 75-2-1104, UCA)

This directive is made this _____ day of _____, 19____.

1. I, _____, being of sound mind, willfully and voluntarily make known my desire that my life not be artificially prolonged by life-sustaining procedures except as I may otherwise provide in this directive.

2. I declare that if at any time I should have an injury, disease, or illness, which is certified in writing to be a terminal condition or persistent vegetative state by two physicians who have personally examined me, and in the opinion of those physicians the application of life-sustaining procedures would serve only to unnaturally prolong the moment of my death and to unnaturally postpone or prolong the dying process, I direct that these procedures be withheld or withdrawn and my death be permitted to occur naturally.

3. I expressly intend this directive to be a final expression of my legal right to refuse medical or surgical treatment and to accept the consequences from this refusal which shall remain in effect notwithstanding my future inability to give current medical directions to treating physicians and other providers of medical services.

4. I understand that the term "life-sustaining procedure" includes artificial nutrition and hydration and any other procedures that I specify below to be considered life-sustaining but does not include the administration of medication or the performance of any medical procedure which is intended to provide comfort care or to alleviate pain:_____

5. I reserve the right to give current medical directions to physicians and other providers of medical services so long as I am able, even though these directions may conflict with the above written directive that life-sustaining procedures be withheld or withdrawn.

6. I understand the full import of this directive and declare that I am emotionally and mentally competent to make this directive.

_____   _____
Declarant's signature   City, County, and State of Residence

We witnesses certify that each of us is 18 years of age or older and each personally witnessed the declarant sign or direct the signing of this directive; that we are acquainted with the declarant and believe him to be of sound mind; that the declarant's desires are as expressed above; that neither of us is a person who signed the above directive on behalf of the declarant; that we are not related to the declarant by blood or marriage nor are we entitled to any portion of declarant's estate according to the laws of intestate succession of this state or under any will or codicil of declarant; that we are not directly financially responsible for declarant's medical care; and that we are not agents of any health care facility in which the declarant may be a patient at the time of signing this directive.

_____   _____
Signature of Witness   Signature of Witness

_____   _____
Address of Witness   Address of Witness

TERMINAL CARE DOCUMENT

To my family, my physician, my lawyer, my clergyman. To any medical facility in whose care I happen to be. To any individual who may become responsible for my health, welfare or affairs.

Death is as much a reality as birth, growth, maturity and old age—it is the one certainty of life. If the time comes when I, _____, can no longer take part in decisions of my own future, let this statement stand as an expression of my wishes, while I am still of sound mind.

If the situation should arise in which I am in a terminal state and there is no reasonable expectation of my recovery, I direct that I be allowed to die a natural death and that my life not be prolonged by extraordinary measures. I do, however, ask that medication be mercifully administered to me to alleviate suffering even though this may shorten my remaining life.

This statement is made after careful consideration and is in accordance with my strong convictions and beliefs. I want the wishes and directions here expressed carried out to the extent permitted by law. Insofar as they are not legally enforceable, I hope that those to whom this will is addressed will regard themselves as morally bound by these provisions.

Signed:_____

Date:_____

Witness:_____

Witness:_____

Copies of this request have been given to:

_____

_____

_____

ADVANCE MEDICAL DIRECTIVE

I, _____, willfully and voluntarily make known my desire and hereby declare:

If at any time my attending physician should determine that I have a terminal condition where the application of life-prolonging procedures would serve only to artificially prolong the dying process, I direct that such procedures be withheld or withdrawn, and that I be permitted to die naturally with only the administration of medication or the performance of any medical procedure deemed necessary to provide me with comfort care or to alleviate pain (OPTION: I specifically direct that the following procedures or treatments be provided to me:_____
_____)

In the absence of my ability to give directions regarding the use of such life-prolonging procedures, it is my intention that this advance directive shall be honored by my family and physician as the final expression of my legal right to refuse medical or surgical treatment and accept the consequences of such refusal.

OPTION: APPOINTMENT OF AGENT (CROSS THROUGH IF YOU DO NOT WANT TO APPOINT AN AGENT TO MAKE HEALTH CARE DECISIONS FOR YOU.)

I hereby appoint _____ (primary agent), of _____
_____ (address and telephone number), as my agent to make health care decisions on my behalf as authorized in this document. If _____ (primary agent) is not reasonably available or is unable or unwilling to act as my agent, then I appoint _____ (successor agent), of
_____ (address and telephone number), to serve in that capacity.

I hereby grant to my agent, named above, full power and authority to make health care decisions on my behalf as described below whenever I have been determined to be incapable of making an informed decision about providing, withholding or withdrawing, medical treatment. The phrase "incapable of making an informed decision" means unable to understand the nature, extent and probably consequences of a proposed medical decision or unable to make a rational evaluation of the risks and benefits of a proposed medical decision as compared with the risks and benefits of alternatives to that decision, or unable to communicate such understanding in any way. My agent's authority hereunder is effective as long as I am incapable of making an informed decision.

The determination that I am incapable of making an informed decision shall be made by my attending physician and a second physician or licensed clinical psychologist after a personal examination of me and shall be certified in writing. Such certification shall be required before treatment is withheld or withdrawn, and before, or as soon as reasonably practicable after, treatment is provided, and every 180 days thereafter while the treatment continues.

In exercising the power to make health care decisions on my behalf, my agent shall follow my desires and preferences as stated in this document or as otherwise known to my agent. My agent shall be guided by my medical diagnosis and prognosis and any information provided by my physicians as to the intrusiveness, pain, risks, and side effects associated with treatment or nontreatment. My agent shall not authorize a course of treatment which he knows, or upon reasonable inquiry ought to know, is contrary to my religious beliefs or my basic values, whether expressed orally or in writing. If my agent cannot determine what treatment choice I would have made on my own behalf, then my agent shall make a choice for me based upon what he believes to be in my best interests.

OPTION: POWERS OF MY AGENT (CROSS THROUGH ANY LANGUAGE YOU DO NOT WANT AND ADD ANY LANGUAGE YOU DO WANT.)

The powers of my agent shall include the following:

A. To consent to or refuse or withdraw consent to any type of medical care, treatment, surgical procedure, diagnostic procedure, medication and the use of mechanical or other procedures that affect any bodily function, including, but not limited to , artificial respiration, artificially administered nutrition and hydration, and cardiopulmonary resuscitation. This authorization specifically includes the power to consent to the administration of dosages of pain relieving medication in excess of standard doses in an amount sufficient to relieve pain, even if such medication carries the risk of addiction or inadvertently hastens my death;

B. To request, receive, and review any information, verbal or written, regarding my physical or mental health, including, but not limited to, medical and hospital records, and to consent to the disclosure of this information;

C. To employ and discharge my health care providers;

D. To authorize my admission to or discharge (including transfer to another facility) from any hospital, hospice, nursing home, adult home or other medical care facility; and

E. To take any lawful actions that may be necessary to carry out these decisions, including the granting of releases of liability to medical providers.

Further, my agent shall not be liable for the costs of treatment pursuant to his authorization, based solely on that authorization.

This advance directive shall not terminate in the event of my disability.

By signing below, I indicate that I am emotionally and mentally competent to make this advance directive and that I understand the purpose and effect of this document.

_____   _____
(Date)   (Signature of Declarant)

The declarant signed the foregoing advance directive in my presence. I am not the spouse or a blood relative of the declarant.

(Witness) _____   (Witness) _____

HEALTH CARE DIRECTIVE

Directive made this _____ day of _____ (month, year).

I, _____, having the capacity to make health care decisions, willfully, and voluntarily make known my desire that my dying shall not be artificially prolonged under the circumstances set forth below, and do hereby declare that:

(a) If at any time I should be diagnosed in writing to be in a terminal condition by the attending physician, or in a permanent unconscious condition by two physicians, and where the application of life-sustaining treatment would serve only to artificially prolong the process of my dying, I direct that such treatment be withheld or withdrawn, and that I be permitted to die naturally. I understand by using this form that a terminal condition means an incurable and irreversible condition caused by injury, disease, or illness, that would within reasonable medical judgment cause death within a reasonable period of time in accordance with accepted medical standards, and where the application of life-sustaining treatment would serve only to prolong the process of dying. I further understand in using this form that a permanent unconscious condition means an incurable and irreversible condition in which I am medically assess within reasonable medical judgment as having no reasonable probability of recovery from an irreversible coma or a persistent vegetative state.

(b) In the absence of my ability to give directions regarding the use of such life-sustaining treatment, it is my intention that this directive shall be honored by my family and physician(s) as the final expression of my legal right to refuse medical or surgical treatment and I accept the consequences of such refusal. If another person is appointed to make these decisions for me, whether through a durable power of attorney or otherwise, I request that the person be guided by this directive and any other clear expressions of my desires.

(c) If I am diagnosed to be in a terminal condition or a permanent unconscious condition (check one):
_____ I DO want to have artificially provided nutrition and hydration.
_____ I DO NOT want to have artificially provided nutrition and hydration.

(d) If I have been diagnosed as pregnant and that diagnosis is known to my physician, this directive shall have no force or effect during the course of my pregnancy.

(e) I understand the full import of this directive and I am emotionally and mentally capable to make the health care decisions contained in this directive.

(f) I understand that before I sign this directive, I can add to or delete from or otherwise change the wording of this directive and that I may add to or delete from this directive at any time and that any changes shall be consistent with Washington state law or federal constitutional law to be legally valid.

(g) It is my wish that every part of this directive be fully implemented. If for any reason any part is held invalid it is my wish that the remainder of my directive be implemented.

Signed_____

_____
City, County, and State of Residence

The declarer has been personally known to me and I believe him or her to be capable of making health care decisions.

Witness_____

Witness_____

LIVING WILL

Living will made this _____ day of _____ (month, year).

I, _____, being of sound mind, willfully and voluntarily declare that in the absence of my ability to give directions regarding the use of life-prolonging intervention, it is my desire that my dying shall not be artificially prolonged under the following circumstances:

If at any time I should be certified by two physicians who have personally examined me, one of whom is my attending physician, to have a terminal condition or to be in a persistent vegetative state, I direct that life-prolonging intervention that would serve solely to artificially prolong the dying process or maintain me in a persistent vegetative state be withheld or withdrawn, and that I be permitted to die naturally with only the administration of medication or the performance of any other medical procedure deemed necessary to keep me comfortable and alleviate pain.

SPECIAL DIRECTIVES OR LIMITATIONS ON THIS DECLARATION:
(If none, write "none")_____
_____

It is my intention that this living will be honored as the final expression of my legal right to refuse medical or surgical treatment and accept the consequences resulting from such refusal.

I understand the full import of this living will.

Signed_____

Address_____

_____

I did not sign the declarant's signature above for or at the direction of the declarant. I am at least eighteen years of age and am not related to the declarant by blood or marriage, entitled to any portion of the estate of the declarant according to the laws of intestate succession of the state of the declarant's domicile or to the best of my knowledge under any will of declarant or codicil thereto, or directly financially responsible for declarant's medical care. I am not the declarant's attending physician or the declarant's health care representative, proxy or successor health care representative under a medical power of attorney.

Witness_____

Address_____

_____

Witness_____

Address_____

_____

STATE OF _____,

COUNTY OF _____,

The foregoing instrument was acknowledged before me this _____ (date) by the declarant and the two witnesses whose signatures appear above.

My commission expires:_____

_____
Signature of Notary Public

DECLARATION TO PHYSICIANS

1. I, _____, being of sound mind, voluntarily state my desire that my dying may not be prolonged under the circumstances specified in this document. Under those circumstances, I direct that I be permitted to die naturally. If I am unable to give directions regarding the use of life-sustaining procedures or feeding tubes, I intend that my family and physician honor this document as the final expression of my legal right to refuse medical or surgical treatment and to accept the consequences from this refusal.

2. If I have a TERMINAL CONDITION, as determined by 2 physicians who have personally examined me, I do not want my dying to be artificially prolonged and I do not want life-sustaining procedures to be used. In addition, if I have such a terminal condition, the following are my directions regarding the use of feeding tubes (check only one):

      a. Use feeding tubes if I have a terminal condition

      b. Do not use feeding tubes if I have a terminal condition

      c. If I have not checked either box, feeding tubes will be used.

3. If I am in a PERSISTENT VEGETATIVE STATE, as determined by 2 physicians who have personally examined me, the following are my directions regarding the use of life-sustaining procedures and feeding tubes:

    a. Check only one:

      Use life-sustaining procedures if I am in a persistent vegetative state

      Do not use life-sustaining procedures if I am in a persistent vegetative state

      If I have not checked either box, life-sustaining procedures will be used.

    b. Check only one:

      Use feeding tubes if I am in a persistent vegetative state

      Do not use feeding tubes if I am in a persistent vegetative state

      If I have not checked either box, feeding tubes will be used.

4. By law, this document cannot be used to authorize: a) withholding or withdrawal of any medication, procedure or feeding tube if to do so would cause me pain or reduce my comfort; and b) withholding or withdrawal of nutrition or hydration that is administered to me through means other than a feeding tube unless, in my physician's opinion, this administration is medically contraindicated.

5. If I have been diagnosed as pregnant and my physician knows of this diagnosis, this document has no effect during the course of my pregnancy.

Signed_____ Date_____

Address_____

I know the person signing this document personally and I believe him or her to be of sound mind. I am not related to the person signing this document by blood, marriage or adoption, and am not entitled to and do not have a claim on any portion of the person's estate and am not otherwise restricted by law from being a witness.

Witness_____

Witness_____

This document is executed as provided in chapter 154, Wisconsin Statutes.

DECLARATION

NOTICE

This document has significant medical, legal and possible ethical implications and effects. Before you sign this document, you should become completely familiar with these implications and effects. The operation, effects and implications of this document may be discussed with a physician, a lawyer, and a clergyman of your choice.

Declaration made this _____ day of _____ (month, year). I,_____, being of sound mind, willfully and voluntarily make known my desire that my dying shall not be artificially prolonged under the circumstances set forth below, do hereby declare:

If at any time I should have an incurable injury, disease or other illness certified to be a terminal condition by two (2) physicians who have personally examined me, one (1) of whom shall be my attending physician, and the physicians have determined that my death will occur whether or not life-sustaining procedures are utilized and where the application of life-sustaining procedures would serve only to artificially prolong the dying process, I direct that such procedures be withheld or withdrawn, and that I be permitted to die naturally with only the administration of medication or the performance of any medical procedure deemed necessary to provide me with comfort care.

If, in spite of this declaration, I am comatose or otherwise unable to make treatment decisions for myself, I HEREBY designate _____to make treatment decisions for me.

In the absence of my ability to give directions regarding the use of life-sustaining procedures, it is my intention that this declaration shall be honored by my family and physician(s) and agent as the final expression of my legal right to refuse medical or surgical treatment and accept the consequences from this refusal. I understand the full import or this declaration and I am emotionally and mentally competent to make this declaration.

Signed_____

City, County and State of Residence_____

The declarant has been personally known to me and I believe him or her to be of sound mind. I did not sign the declarant's signature above for or at the direction of the declarant. I am not related to the declarant by blood or marriage, entitled to any portion of the estate of the declarant according to the laws of intestate succession or under any will of the declarant or codicil thereto, or directly financially responsible for declarant's medical care.

Witness_____

Witness_____

STATEMENT OF DESIRES AND LOCATION OF PROPERTY & DOCUMENTS

I, _____, am signing this document as the expression of my desires as to the matters stated below, and to inform my family members or other significant persons of the location of certain property and documents in the event of any emergency or of my death.

1. **Funeral Desires.** It is my desire that the following arrangements be made for my funeral and disposition of remains in the event of my death (state if you have made any arrangements, such as pre-paid burial plans, cemetery plots owned, etc.):

    o   Burial at _____
        _____.

    o   Cremation at _____
        _____.

    o   Other specific desires: _____
        _____
        _____.

2. **Minor Children.** I have the following minor child(ren): _____
    _____. The following are my desires
    concerning the custody, education, and rearing of said minor child(ren): _____
    _____
    _____
    _____
    _____
    _____.

3. **Pets.** I have the following pet(s): _____
    _____. The following are my desires
    concerning the care of said pet(s): _____
    _____
    _____.

4. **Notification.** I would like the following person(s) notified in the event of emergency or death (give name, address and phone number):

    _____
    _____
    _____
    _____
    _____.

5. **Location of Documents.** The following is a list of important documents, and their location:

- Last Will and Testament, dated _____. Location: _____

  _____.

- Durable Power of Attorney, dated _____. Location: _____

  _____.

- Living Will, dated _____. Location: _____

  _____.

- Deed(s) to real estate (describe property location and location of deed):

  _____

  _____

  _____

- Title(s) to vehicles (cars, boats, etc.) (Describe vehicle, its location, and location of title, registration, or other documents):

  _____

  _____

  _____

  _____

- Life insurance policies (list name address & phone number of insurance company and insurance agent, policy number, and location of policy):

  _____

  _____

  _____

- Other insurance policies (list type, company & agent, policy number, and location of policy):

  _____

  _____

  _____

  _____

o   Other: (list other documents such as stock certificates, bonds, certificates of deposit, etc., and their location):

_____

_____

_____

_____

6.   **Location of Assets.** In addition to items readily visible in my home or listed above, I have the following assets:

o   Safe deposit box located at _____, box number _____.

Key located at: _____.

o   Bank accounts (list name & address of bank, type of account, and account number):

_____

o   Other (describe the item and give its location):

_____

_____

_____

_____

_____

_____

7.   Other desires or information (state any desires or provide any information not given above; use additional sheets of paper if necessary):

_____

_____

_____

_____

_____

Dated: _____

_____

Signature

STANDARD NOTARY PAGE

State of _____)

County of _____)

    On this _____ day of _____, 19_____, before me, personally appeared _____, principal, and _____ and _____, witnesses, who are personally known to me or who provided _____ _____ as identification, and signed the foregoing instrument in my presence.

_____

Notary Public

My Commission expires:

ADDENDUM TO LIVING WILL

I, _____, hereby execute this addendum to the _____ ("my living will"), executed by me on _____, 19_____. The sole purpose of this addendum is to more fully express my wishes regarding my medical treatment. If any or all of the terms of this addendum are determined to be invalid, my living will shall remain in effect. My desires regarding my medical care and treatment are as indicated below:

_____ 1. If I should have an incurable or irreversible condition that will cause my death within a relatively short time without the administration of artificial life support procedures or treatment, and if I am unable to make decisions regarding my medical treatment, I direct my attending physician to withhold or withdraw procedures that merely prolong the dying process and are not necessary to my comfort or to alleviate pain, even if such pain medication hastens death. This authorization includes, but is not limited to, the withholding or withdrawal of the following types of medical treatment (subject to any special instructions in paragraph 5 below):

       _____ a. Artificial feeding and hydration.
       _____ b. Cardiopulmonary resuscitation (this includes, but is not limited to, the use of drugs, electric shock, and artificial breathing).
       _____ c. Kidney dialysis.
       _____ d. Surgery or other invasive procedures.
       _____ e. Antibiotics.
       _____ f. Other: _____
       _____

_____ 2. If I should be in an irreversible coma or persistent vegetative state that my physicians reasonably believe to be irreversible or incurable, I direct my attending physicians to withhold or withdraw medical procedures and treatment other than such medical procedures and treatment necessary to my comfort or to alleviate pain, even if such pain medication hastens death This authorization includes, but is not limited to, the withholding or withdrawal of the following types of medical treatment (subject to any special instructions in paragraph 4 below):

       _____ a. Artificial feeding and hydration.
       _____ b. Cardiopulmonary resuscitation (this includes, but is not limited to, the use of drugs, electric shock, and artificial breathing).
       _____ c. Kidney dialysis.
       _____ d. Surgery or other invasive procedures.
       _____ e. Antibiotics.
       _____ f. Other: _____
       _____

_____ 3. If I should have a medical condition where I am unable to communicate my desires as to treatment and my physician determines that the burdens of treatment outweigh the expected benefits, I direct my attending physicians to withhold or withdraw medical procedures and treatment other than such medical procedures and treatment necessary to my comfort or to alleviate pain, even if such paid medication hastens death This authorization includes, but is not limited to, the withholding or withdrawal of the following types of medical treatment (subject to any special instructions in paragraph 4 below):

       _____ a. Artificial feeding and hydration.

_____ b. Cardiopulmonary resuscitation (this includes, but is not limited to, the use of drugs, electric shock, and artificial breathing).

_____ c. Kidney dialysis.

_____ d. Surgery or other invasive procedures.

_____ e. Antibiotics.

_____ f. Other: _____
_____

_____ 4. I want my life prolonged to the greatest extent possible (subject to any special instructions in paragraph 4 below).

_____ 5. Special instructions (if any) _____
_____
_____
_____

Signed this _____ day of _____,19_____.

_____
Signature

Address:_____

_____

The declarant is personally known to me and voluntarily signed this document in my presence.

Witness:_____   Witness_____

Name:_____   Name:_____

Address:_____   Address:_____

_____   _____

State of _____)
County of _____)
    On this _____ day of _____, 19_____, before me, personally appeared
_____, principal, and
_____ and _____,
witnesses, who are personally known to me or who provided _____
_____
as identification, and signed the foregoing instrument in my presence.

_____
Notary Public
My Commission expires:

INDEX

Your #1 Source for Real World Legal Information...

LEGAL SURVIVAL GUIDES™

- Written by lawyers
- Simple English explanation of the law
- Forms and instructions included

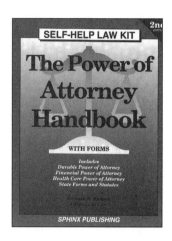 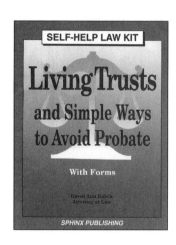 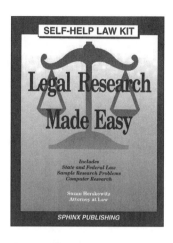

THE POWER OF ATTORNEY HANDBOOK (2ND EDITION)

It is now easier than ever to authorize someone to act on your behalf for your convenience or necessity. Forms with instructions are included, as well as a state-by-state reference guide to power of attorney laws.

140 pages; $19.95;
ISBN 1-57248-044-0

LIVING TRUSTS AND SIMPLE WAYS TO AVOID PROBATE

What everyone needs to know about probate and who needs to avoid it. Included are forms for creating your own living trust without a lawyer. Even if you don't use a trust, this book can save hundreds of dollars in lawyer and probate fees.

140 pages; $19.95;
ISBN 1-57248-019-X

LEGAL RESEARCH MADE EASY

This book for non-lawyers explains how to use the various types of legal reference books such as legal encyclopedias, statutes, digests, American Law Reports, and Shepard's Citations, as well as computerized legal databases. Includes state and federal materials.

124 pages; $14.95;
ISBN 1-57248-008-4

What our customers say about our books:

"It couldn't be more clear for the lay person." —R.D.

"I want you to know I really appreciate your book. It has saved me a lot of time and money." —L.T.

"Your real estate contracts book has saved me nearly $12,000.00 in closing costs over the past year." —A.B.

"...many of the legal questions that I have had over the years were answered clearly and concisely through your plain English interpretation of the law." —C.E.H.

"If there weren't people out there like you I'd be lost. You have the best books of this type out there." —S.B.

"...your forms and directions are easy to follow." —C.V.M.

Legal Survival Guides are directly available from the publisher, or from your local bookstores.
For credit card orders call 1–800–43–BRIGHT, write P.O. Box 372, Naperville, IL 60566,
or fax 630-961-2168

LEGAL SURVIVAL GUIDES™ NATIONAL TITLES
Valid in All 50 States

LEGAL SURVIVAL IN BUSINESS

How to Form Your Own Corporation (2E)	$19.95
How to Register Your Own Copyright (2E)	$19.95
How to Register Your Own Trademark (2E)	$19.95
Most Valuable Business Forms You'll Ever Need	$19.95
Most Valuable Corporate Forms You'll Ever Need	$24.95
Software Law (with diskette)	$29.95

LEGAL SURVIVAL IN COURT

Crime Victim's Guide to Justice	$19.95
Debtors' Rights (2E)	$12.95
Defend Yourself Against Criminal Charges	$19.95
Grandparents' Rights	$19.95
Help Your Lawyer Win Your Case	$12.95
Jurors' Rights	$9.95
Legal Malpractice and Other Claims Against Your Lawyer	$18.95
Legal Research Made Easy	$14.95
Simple Ways to Protect Yourself From Lawsuits	$24.95
Victim's Rights	$12.95
Winning Your Personal Injury Claim	$19.95

LEGAL SURVIVAL IN REAL ESTATE

How to Buy a Condominium or Townhome	$16.95
How to Negotiate Real Estate Contracts (2E)	$16.95
How to Negotiate Real Estate Leases (2E)	$16.95
Successful Real Estate Brokerage Management	$19.95

LEGAL SURVIVAL IN PERSONAL AFFAIRS

How to File Your Own Bankruptcy (4E)	$19.95
How to File Your Own Divorce (3E)	$19.95
How to Make Your Own Will	$12.95
How to Write Your Own Living Will	$9.95
Living Trusts and Simple Ways to Avoid Probate	$19.95
Neighbor vs. Neighbor	$12.95
Power of Attorney Handbook (2E)	$19.95
Social Security Benefits Handbook	$14.95
U.S.A. Immigration Guide (2E)	$19.95
Guia de Inmigracion a Estados Unidos	$19.95

Legal Survival Guides are directly available from the publisher, or from your local bookstores.

For credit card orders call 1–800–43–BRIGHT, write P.O. Box 372, Naperville, IL 60566, or fax 630-961-2168

LEGAL SURVIVAL GUIDES™ STATE TITLES

Up-to-date for Your State

NEW YORK

How to File for Divorce in NY	$19.95
How to Make a NY Will	$12.95
How to Start a Business in NY	$16.95
How to Win in Small Claims Court in NY	$14.95
Landlord's Rights and Duties in NY	$19.95
New York Power of Attorney Handbook	$12.95

PENNSYLVANIA

How to File for Divorce in PA	$19.95
How to Make a PA Will	$12.95
How to Start a Business in PA	$16.95
Landlord's Rights and Duties in PA	$19.95

FLORIDA

Florida Power of Attorney Handbook	$9.95
How to Change Your Name in FL (3E)	$14.95
How to File a FL Construction Lien (2E)	$19.95
How to File a Guardianship in FL	$19.95
How to File for Divorce in FL (4E)	$21.95
How to Form a Nonprofit Corp in FL (3E)	$19.95
How to Form a Simple Corp in FL (3E)	$19.95
How to Make a FL Will (4E)	$9.95
How to Modify Your FL Divorce Judgement (3E)	$22.95
How to Probate an Estate in FL (2E)	$24.95
How to Start a Business in FL (4E)	$16.95
How to Win in Small Claims Court in FL (5E)	$14.95
Land Trusts in FL (4E)	$24.95
Landlord's Rights and Duties in FL (6E)	$19.95
Women's Legal Rights in FL	$19.95

GEORGIA

How to File for Divorce in GA (2E)	$19.95
How to Make a GA Will (2E)	$9.95
How to Start and Run a GA Business (2E)	$18.95

ILLINOIS

How to File for Divorce in IL	$19.95
How to Make an IL Will	$9.95
How to Start a Business in IL	$16.95

MASSACHUSETTS

How to File for Divorce in MA	$19.95
How to Make a MA Will	$9.95
How to Probate an Estate in MA	$19.95
How to Start a Business in MA	$16.95
Landlord's Rights and Duties in MA	$19.95

MICHIGAN

How to File for Divorce in MI	$19.95
How to Make a MI Will	$9.95
How to Start a Business in MI	$16.95

MINNESOTA

How to File for Divorce in MN	$19.95
How to Form a Simple Corporation in MN	$19.95
How to Make a MN Will	$9.95
How to Start a Business in MN	$16.95

NORTH CAROLINA

How to File for Divorce in NC	$19.95
How to Make a NC Will	$9.95
How to Start a Business in NC	$16.95

TEXAS

How to File for Divorce in TX	$19.95
How to Form a Simple Corporation in TX	$19.95
How to Make a TX Will	$9.95
How to Probate an Estate in TX	$19.95
How to Start a Business in TX	$16.95
How to Win in Small Claims Court in TX	$14.95
Landlord's Rights and Duties in TX	$19.95

Legal Survival Guides are directly available from the publisher, or from your local bookstores.

For credit card orders call 1–800–43–BRIGHT, write P.O. Box 372, Naperville, IL 60566, or fax 630-961-2168

Legal Survival Guides™ • Order Form

BILL TO:

SHIP TO:

| Phone # | Terms | F.O.B. Chicago, IL | Ship Date |

Charge my:

☐ VISA   ☐ Mastercard   ☐ American Express

☐ **Money Order** (no personal checks please)

Credit Card Number

Expiration Date

Qty	ISBN	Title	Retail
		Legal Survival Guides Fall 97 National Frontlist	
	1-57071-223-9	How to File Your Own Bankruptcy (4E)	$19.95
	1-57071-224-7	How to File Your Own Divorce (3E)	$19.95
	1-57071-227-1	How to Form Your Own Corporation (2E)	$19.95
	1-57071-228-X	How to Make Your Own Will	$12.95
	1-57071-225-5	How to Register Your Own Copyright (2E)	$19.95
	1-57071-226-3	How to Register Your Own Trademark (2E)	$19.95
		Fall 97 New York Frontlist	
	1-57071-184-4	How to File for Divorce in NY	$19.95
	1-57071-183-6	How to Make a NY Will	$12.95
	1-57071-185-2	How to Start a Business in NY	$16.95
	1-57071-187-9	How to Win in Small Claims Court in NY	$14.95
	1-57071-186-0	Landlord's Rights and Duties in NY	$19.95
	1-57071-188-7	New York Power of Attorney Handbook	$12.95
		Fall 97 Pennsylvania Frontlist	
	1-57071-177-1	How to File for Divorce in PA	$19.95
	1-57071-176-3	How to Make a PA Will	$12.95
	1-57071-178-X	How to Start a Business in PA	$16.95
	1-57071-179-8	Landlord's Rights and Duties in PA	$19.95
		Legal Survival Guides National Backlist	
	1-57071-166-6	Crime Victim's Guide to Justice	$19.95
	1-57248-023-8	Debtors' Rights (2E)	$12.95
	1-57071-162-3	Defend Yourself Against Criminal Charges	$19.95
	1-57248-001-7	Grandparents' Rights	$19.95
	0-913825-99-9	Guia de Inmigracion a Estados Unidos	$19.95
	1-57248-021-1	Help Your Lawyer Win Your Case	$12.95
	1-57071-164-X	How to Buy a Condominium or Townhome	$16.95
	1-57248-035-1	How to Negotiate Real Estate Contracts (2E)	$16.95
	1-57248-036-X	How to Negotiate Real Estate Leases (2E)	$16.95
	1-57071-167-4	How to Write Your Own Living Will	$9.95
	1-57248-031-9	Jurors' Rights	$9.95
	1-57248-032-7	Legal Malpractice and Other Claims Against Your Lawyer	$18.95
	1-57248-008-4	Legal Research Made Easy	$14.95
	1-57248-019-X	Living Trusts and Simple Ways to Avoid Probate	$19.95
	1-57248-022-X	Most Valuable Business Forms You'll Ever Need	$19.95
	1-57248-007-6	Most Valuable Corporate Forms You'll Ever Need	$24.95
	0-913825-41-7	Neighbor vs. Neighbor	$12.95
	1-57248-044-0	Power of Attorney Handbook (2E)	$19.95
	1-57248-020-3	Simple Ways to Protect Yourself From Lawsuits	$24.95
	1-57248-033-5	Social Security Benefits Handbook	$14.95
	1-57071-163-1	Software Law (w/diskette)	$29.95
	0-913825-86-7	Successful Real Estate Brokerage Mgmt.	$19.95
	1-57248-000-9	U.S.A. Immigration Guide (2E)	$19.95
	0-913825-82-4	Victim's Rights	$12.95
	1-57071-165-8	Winning Your Personal Injury Claim	$19.95
		Florida Backlist	
	0-913825-81-6	Florida Power of Attorney Handbook	$9.95
	1-57248-028-9	How to Change Your Name in FL (3E)	$14.95
	0-913825-84-0	How to File a FL Construction Lien (2E)	$19.95
	0-913825-53-0	How to File a Guardianship in FL	$19.95
	1-57248-046-7	How to File for Divorce in FL (4E)	$21.95

Qty	ISBN	Title	Retail
		Florida Backlist (cont')	
	1-57248-004-1	How to Form a Nonprofit Corp in FL (3E)	$19.95
	0-913825-96-4	How to Form a Simple Corp in FL (3E)	$19.95
	1-57248-027-0	How to Make a FL Will (4E)	$9.95
	1-57248-056-4	How to Modify Your FL Divorce Judgement (3E)	$22.95
	1-57248-003-3	How to Probate an Estate in FL (2E)	$24.95
	1-57248-005-X	How to Start a Business in FL (4E)	$16.95
	0-913825-97-2	How to Win in Small Claims Court in FL (5E)	$14.95
	1-57248-029-7	Land Trusts in FL (4E)	$24.95
	1-57248-057-2	Landlord's Rights and Duties in FL (6E)	$19.95
	0-913825-73-5	Women's Legal Rights in FL	$19.95
		Georgia Backlist	
	1-57248-058-0	How to File for Divorce in GA (2E)	$19.95
	1-57248-047-5	How to Make a GA Will (2E)	$9.95
	1-57248-026-2	How to Start and Run a GA Business (2E)	$18.95
		Illinois Backlist	
	1-57248-042-4	How to File for Divorce in IL	$19.95
	1-57248-043-2	How to Make an IL Will	$9.95
	1-57248-041-6	How to Start a Business in IL	$16.95
		Massachusetts Backlist	
	1-57248-051-3	How to File for Divorce in MA	$19.95
	1-57248-050-5	How to Make a MA Will	$9.95
	1-57248-053-X	How to Probate an Estate in MA	$19.95
	1-57248-054-8	How to Start a Business in MA	$16.95
	1-57248-055-6	Landlord's Rights and Duties in MA	$19.95
		Michigan Backlist	
	1-57248-014-9	How to File for Divorce in MI	$19.95
	1-57248-015-7	How to Make a MI Will	$9.95
	1-57248-013-0	How to Start a Business in MI	$16.95
		Minnesota Backlist	
	1-57248-039-4	How to File for Divorce in MN	$19.95
	1-57248-040-8	How to Form a Simple Corporation in MN	$19.95
	1-57248-037-8	How to Make a MN Will	$9.95
	1-57248-038-6	How to Start a Business in MN	$16.95
		North Carolina Backlist	
	0-913825-94-8	How to File for Divorce in NC	$19.95
	0-913825-92-1	How to Make a NC Will	$9.95
	0-913825-93-X	How to Start a Business in NC	$16.95
		Texas Backlist	
	0-913825-91-3	How to File for Divorce in TX	$19.95
	1-57248-009-2	How to Form a Simple Corporation in TX	$19.95
	0-913825-89-1	How to Make a TX Will	$9.95
	1-57248-010-6	How to Probate an Estate in TX	$19.95
	0-913825-90-5	How to Start a Business in TX	$16.95
	1-57248-012-2	How to Win in Small Claims Court in TX	$14.95
	1-57248-011-4	Landlord's Rights and Duties in TX	$19.95
		SUBTOTAL	
		IL Residents add 6.75%, FL Residents add county sales tax	
		Shipping— $4.00 for 1st book, $1.00 each additional	
		Total	

To order, call Sourcebooks at 1-800-43-BRIGHT or FAX (630)961-2168 (Bookstores, libraries, wholesalers—please call for discount)